Allan Smithee (perhaps not his real name) has worked in the film business for nearly 15 years. As a publicist he has orchestrated distribution campaigns for well over 60 movies and has on-screen credits as unit publicist for more than 20 feature productions. A member of the British Academy of Film and Television, he currently develops scripts for a wide range of production companies and film bodies as well as consulting for diverse clients including Film London (the city's film body). He has worked with Al Pacino, Dennis Hopper, Kevin Costner, Mike Leigh and three of All Saints!

101

MOVIES
TO AVOID

THE MOST
OVERRATED
FILMS EVER!

ALLAN SMITHEE

CYAN

First published in 2006 by

Cyan Communications Limited
119 Wardour Street, London W1F 0UW
United Kingdom
T: +44 (0)20 7565 6120
E: sales@cyanbooks.com
www.cyanbooks.com

A CIP record for this book is available from the British Library

ISBN-13 978-1-905736-06-5
ISBN-10 1-905736-06-1

Printed and bound in Great Britain by
TJ International Ltd, Padstow, Cornwall

For my poor long-suffering wife Ruth, who's had to sit
through so many rubbish movies with me!

And special thanks to Janey. Ms Burton – you're a great
editor who suffered my bad grammar, terrible spelling and
overuse of exclamation marks with remarkable patience!!!

Contents

Introduction

The first thing to get straight is that this is not a list of the 101 worst movies. That, sadly, would be too hard to narrow down. And no one goes out to make a bad movie. I bet even the illustrious Alan Metter (director of that classic, *Police Academy 7: Mission to Moscow*) went about his task with gusto and enthusiasm, trying to make the best movie possible (Alan – sorry mate, you failed). But we're not going to consider the likes of *My Stepmother is an Alien*, or even *The Next Best Thing*, here. Our intention is not to kick a dog when it's down, but when it's up on its hind legs and pretending to be a thoroughbred.

This is a collection of the movies that people (especially those damned critics) have told you are really, really good – classics in their genre. Then you spend the money and find you've wasted two hours of your important time. Well, fear no more. With this concise but informative (and opinionated) tome you'll never have to sit through another well-reviewed stinker again. We hope to steer you away from the pompous, the pretentious and the downright horrific wastes of celluloid that have for some reason become known as "classic movies."

You have to wonder how some of these ever reached such heady heights in the first place. The first people to name and shame for this appalling state of affairs have to be the critics. These leeches never queue for a movie in the rain, or have to pay for their popcorn. For the most part they see films in small screening rooms during the daytime when real moviegoers are out earning the admission price. This obviously warps their view. They're not seeing the picture in the same environment (or even at the same time of day) that you're likely to, and so their views are largely irrelevant. It's a bit like someone going to your favorite vacation destination during the hurricane season: although it's exactly the same place they are not going to have the same experience as you will.

The second point that has to be noted about critics is that they go to see the previews with their peers. If you've ever met a film critic you will spot one thing straight away: they do not like to look silly (quite a few of them fail). Their job is to berate and belittle, and because of this they have an inside knowledge of the pain that criticism can cause. Thus they are loath to receive their own medicine. And so, when they watch a film they're always wondering what the other guys are thinking. One guffaw, and the rest will join in. A slight giggle will soon turn into a crescendo of raucous laughter. And then they go for a coffee (although at times it appears they're drinking something a lot stronger) and will openly discuss "their views" with the other critics. Never has the emperor worn fewer clothes!

The other problem is your own friends. I bet you've spent many an unhappy night in a movie theatre thinking "What did Jack see in this pile of rubbish?" The answer for the most part is that he probably didn't even see it. We all love to drone on and seem knowledgeable about the cinema. People will quite happily put their hands up and admit to not reading a book for years, or being baffled by art. They might even admit to preferring Andrew Lloyd Webber to Shakespeare. But cinema is the artform of the moment. You can't be seen to not know what's hot and what's a classic, so you make it up. Yes. I'm sorry to break it to you. But your best friend hasn't seen *Battleship Potemkin* (or, giving it its original Russian title, *Bronenosets Potyomkin* as I like to call it ... no, of course I don't). They probably haven't even see *La Dolce Vita* (or *La Dolce Vita* as I ...). Truth be known, they're much happier watching *Wimbledon* (Kirsten Dunst in a tennis skirt – how could it possibly go wrong?) and can tell you the exact moment in *The Woman in Red* that Kelly Le Brock goes full frontal. But they're not going to tell you that, so they warble on about the dark intensity of Kieslowski and the edgy genius of early Peter Jackson. Take it on the chin buddy – you've been conned!

But no more. No longer will you come out of a cinema thinking "was it just me, or did that not make sense?" *101 Movies to Avoid* is a list of the most lauded piles of garbage ever seen in a cinema (or on a television). It could be the start of a whole new honesty about film. Just because it's about the holocaust doesn't mean that it should win an Oscar (hang your head in shame Roman Polanski). No rear was meant to be immobile for three hours in the company of strangers – if they can't tell their story in 90 minutes maybe it's them that's wrong, not us. Hopefully this humble collection of vitriol will spur you into standing your ground, and enjoying movies because they are actually good rather than because everyone says that they're good. Who knows? You might even start to appreciate the maligned work of Alan Metter.

Like everything, the list is purely subjective – a voice in the wilderness against undeserved critical acclaim. If you don't agree, please let me know. The book will be updated yearly, and so your input is important (although if you don't agree with me I'll probably ignore you. We all have our egos you know). There might also be other little gems that have escaped me. Stories about traveling for hours in the snow to see an acclaimed classic, only to spend two hours looking through the glasses worn by the man in front to see if he was long or short sighted.

Also, six or seven new movies come out every week. Those distinguished members of the American Academy will award new garlands each year to the films they think will least upset anyone. So there will be plenty of newcomers trying to push their way onto the list. Agree, disagree or contribute to allan.smithee@cyanbooks.com. We may even organize some form of raffle – first prize a copy of *2001: A Space Odyssey* … second prize two copies of *2001: A Space Odyssey*.

THE MOVIES

24 7: Twenty Four Seven

Two rival gangs are brought together, and given something to believe in, by an eccentric local boxing coach.

Director	Shane Meadows
Writers	Shane Meadows, Paul Fraser
Starring	Danny Nussbaum
	Bob Hoskins
	Bruce Jones
	Annette Badland
Released	1997
Awards	FIPRESCI prize at Venice Film Festival, Best Actor (Bob Hoskins) European Film Awards, Douglas Hickox Award at British Independent Film Awards, nominated for Best British Film BAFTA.
Box office	Worldwide US$ figure unavailable

"Shot beautifully, Meadows's film is a typically witty look at disenchantment, redemption, and regret … peppered with flashes of brilliant humour and candid, unlikely beauty, it's an engaging and outwardly confident blend of authentic naturalism and low-budget inventiveness." David Wood, BBCi

Shane Meadows has gone on to make two of the best British films of recent times – *A Room for Romeo Brass* (1999) and *Dead Man's Shoes* (2004), so we shouldn't be too hard on this effort. But it really is a film that sums up the raison d'être of this book. Critics salivated over this "gritty and realistic" film (although I'd like to know how many of them actually were members of boxing clubs in Nottingham to make them such experts). Pretentious people at dinner parties waxed lyrical about its "ethereal beauty" (Bob Hoskins? Beautiful? Anyone who saw his full frontal nude scene in *Mrs. Henderson Presents* may just disagree).

Thankfully, in this case, not many of the general public were duped (it bombed at the box office). Perhaps my main gripe is that the movie is in black and white. Why? There seemed no purpose for this arty device. Many lauded *24 7* for being so realistic – they should go to the optician. I see colours out my window, not monochrome. If a film wants to visually bring over the impression of drabness they can do it subtly and inventively by the use of colours in both the production and costume design. To simply shoot the thing in black and white is a cop-out that makes the whole thing feel artificial (and arty). Realistic? Pah!

Added to this Meadows uses "real kids" who have never acted before. I wouldn't pay full price to see a game of amateur football, so why am I expected to buy a full cinema ticket to see amateurs acting? That's just cheating.

The story isn't realistic – it only seemed so to uppity critics whose most recent experience of violence was having their bare buttocks roundly smacked at private school (most have had to pay for the pleasure ever since). *24 7* is simplistic and far too convenient.

24 Hour Party People

The story of the "Madchester" music scene when pop impresario Tony Wilson made stars of local groups such as Joy Division and The Happy Mondays.

Director	Michael Winterbottom
Writer	Frank Cottrell Boyce
Starring	Steve Coogan
	Danny Cunningham
	Shirley Henderson
	John Thomson
Released	2002
Awards	British Independent Film Award for Achievement in Production. Nominated for Golden Palm at Cannes, and Best British Film at the Empire Awards.
Box office	Worldwide US$ figure unavailable
Tagline	The unbelievably true story of one man, one movement, the music and madness that was Manchester.

"This is what movies aspire to: *24 Hour Party People* has strong characters who are likable yet fallible, humor that is consistent and uproarious, a dramatic thread that sustains it from start to finish, and an edge – both gritty and ironic – that flatters every scene." Jonathan Curiel, *San Francisco Chronicle*

Ah, the gods of music: The Beatles, The Rolling Stones … The Happy Mondays. Yes, exactly. Manchester in the 1980s spawned a small smattering of reasonably successful "indie" bands (the "movement", for want of a better word, was referred to as "Madchester"). They didn't achieve the sales or following of "Seattle grunge", nor the legendary status of the "Merseyside beat". But for director Michael Winterbottom they were important.

That's fine in itself, we all cling on to our memories of youth. The problem is that Winterbottom apparently deemed that they were equally important to everyone else and decided to make a movie about them. Presumptuous and not a little arrogant, *24 Hour Party People* wholeheartedly believes that everyone watching this movie will instantly recognize the songs, the bands, and the "ever-so-famous" incidents in the life of an obscure regional television presenter who set up an unsuccessful record company.

No Michael – only men in their late thirties who eschewed mainstream music would be able to do this. But guess what? That's exactly the profile of movie financiers, who instantly recognized every smug "hint hint" little joke and every obscure cameo. Not worrying that their music fan contemporaries were now wearing slippers and only visiting the cinema to bring their screaming children to *Pokemon* they decided to waste a heap of British taxpayers' money on a lovefest that interested no one except themselves.

And the problem is that this could have been a good film (preferably without Steve Coogan merely forcing his television persona onto another character). The story itself is bizarre, exciting and very funny. But the filmmakers wholeheartedly refused to make the movie accessible to anyone that wasn't in their gang.

28 Days Later

A man wakes up in hospital to find a virus has ravaged the land, killing most and leaving the rest crazed zombies. Together with a small band of survivors he desperately tries to find safety and normality.

Director	Danny Boyle
Writer	Alex Garland
Starring	Cillian Murphy
	Naomie Harris
	Brendan Gleeson
	Christopher Eccleston
Released	2002/2003
Awards	Won Best British film at the Empire Awards, and Best Cinematography at the European Films Awards. Nominated for three British Independent Film Awards as well as an MTV Award for Best Breakthrough Male Performance.
Box office	Worldwide US$ figure unavailable
Tagline	Be thankful for everything, for soon there will be nothing.

"Outlandishly edge-conscious … unassuming ticket buyers may be spot-welded to their seats with an unfamiliar intensity." Michael Atkinson, *Village Voice*

"When *28 Days Later* is not scaring you silly, it invites you to reflect seriously on the fragility of modern civilization." A. O. Scott, *The New York Times*

It's only when I was researching this that I realized Alex Garland wrote *28 Days Later*. It kinda makes sense (see entry for *The Beach*), as this is yet another mundane pointless exercise that seems to have bamboozled the world's critics.

This is a movie where nothing happens, for no apparent reason. In fact, the scene that everyone lauds is of London completely empty and still. Come on ... take a photograph why don't you? To save you a waste of a butt-numbing two hours let me be the first to break the news: it's not interesting, it's not entertaining, it's not scary, it's not funny (bar a ridiculous cameo from the usually reliable Christopher Eccleston who seems to be playing the Brigadier from TV's *Dr. Who*). There is nothing that engages the emotions, or the intellect for that matter.

The zombies in *Shaun of the Dead* (2004) were scarier and more real (that is, if you know what real zombies look like), the blood and gore have no effect, and the only real horror is the feeling around the hour mark that you're never going to be able to leave the cinema.

There's no real point or goal to *28 Days Later*. We never learn why the main character (Jim) escapes the plague, or virus, or whatever it is; and Jim has little in the way of a goal except to reach Manchester (come on, people from Oldham don't want to go to Manchester).

God, I was bored.

2001: A Space Odyssey

A strange monolith is found on the moon; a space crew (in a ship controlled by a computer called HAL) go to investigate.

Director	Stanley Kubrick
Writers	Stanley Kubrick, Arthur C. Clarke
Starring	Keir Dullea
	Gary Lockwood
	William Sylvester
Released	1968
Awards	Oscar for Best Special Effects. BAFTAs for Art Direction, Soundtrack and Cinematography and a Donatello for Best Foreign Movie. Oscar nominated for Writing, Direction and Art Direction. Nominated for Best Film at the BAFTAs and Directors' Guild.
Box office	$190,700,000 (Worldwide)
Tagline	An epic drama of adventure and exploration.

"*2001* is not concerned with thrilling us, but with inspiring our awe." Roger Ebert, *Chicago Sun-Times*

So we all know that the 1960s were famous for drugs, and if you can remember Mick Jagger you should have another spliff, but what the hell is this movie all about?

There's a big rock, some sort of space mission, a computer with a really annoying voice, nice little dance scene with the planets colliding, and that's it really. No story, no theme, no plot and no good. Rarely has the emperor worn fewer clothes and nobody noticed.

2001 is perhaps the ultimate geeks' movie. Critics were right, Kubrick was ahead of his time with this one. It's only now that millions of sad, lonely, bespectacled sci-fi fans can sit in their bedrooms (proprietor: Mum, of course) and discuss with similarly sweater-wearing dorks the deep meanings behind the film. At last they can hold their greasy-haired heads up high – by basically pretending they've got a clue what this was all about.

Beware oh patient reader, *2001: A Space Odyssey* is the film that always gets you. You've heard about it, people say it's great (please note that those people are either geeks or liars) and you spend your hard-earned money to see yet another re-release. Trust me, it's really not worth it. *The Simpsons* covered most of the memorable scenes (and did them much better) and the rest is just meaningless mumbo-jumbo.

A perfect con trick by Kubrick, who was after all the master of illusion – he nearly made us believe that Tom and Nicole were in love in *Eyes Wide Shut*. Catch the right moment, when the world is stoned, and tell them that your film is deep and meaningful. Hey presto – huge hit, with many going again and again (because they couldn't remember it). Everyone happy.

American Beauty

Suburb-dwelling Lester is having a mid-life crisis; spurred on by an infatuation for one of his daughter's friends he begins to unravel his "perfect, American dream" life.

Director	Sam Mendes
Writer	Alan Ball
Starring	Kevin Spacey
	Annette Bening
	Thora Birch
	Wes Bentley
Released	1999
Awards	Oscars for Best Actor, Best Director, Best Picture, Best Writing, Cinematography. BAFTAs for Best Actor, Actress, Film, Editing and Cinematography. Golden Globes for Best Picture, Direction and Screenplay and lots more. Oscar nominated for Best Actress, Editing and Music; BAFTA nominated for Direction, Supporting Actress (two), Supporting Actor, Editing
Box office	$356,296,601 (Worldwide)
Tagline	Look closer.

"Unsettling, unnerving, undefinable … a quirky and disturbing take on modern American life energized by bravura performances from Kevin Spacey and Annette Bening, *American Beauty* is a blood-chilling dark comedy with unexpected moments of both fury and warmth, a strange, brooding and very accomplished film that sets us back on our heels from its opening frames." Kenneth Turan, *LA Times*; metacritic.com

I learnt a lot from *American Beauty*. It's a movie that takes concentration, but if you look close enough you'll discover that Thora Birch's breasts are not the same size, Kevin Spacey is annoying (in every role – how does that happen?) and no matter how slow the DVD player goes you never get to see any of Mena Suvari's important bits. And that's about it really.

A clever illusion of style over content, director Mendes wants us to think that there is more to this movie than meets the eye. There's not. In fact, there's less. It doesn't tell you anything you didn't know about the human psyche, or even modern America. The imagery is intrusive and the narrative refuses to hold together.

Why would anyone think that a "mid-life crisis" is particularly interesting or entertaining? It's dull, meandering and hardly worth taking notice of. The film has a few decent performances, most notably from Annette Bening and Chris Cooper, but overall the characters are stereotypes.

Still, it's always interesting to see an unbalanced pair of breasts make it good in Hollywood.

Angel

Set during the Northern Irish "troubles" a saxophonist in a showband witnesses the cruel murder of his manager and a beautiful mute girl. He goes in search of justice and the truth behind the killings.

Director	Neil Jordan
Writer	Neil Jordan
Starring	Veronica Quilligan
	Stephen Rea
	Alan Devlin
Released	1982
Awards	None
Box office	Worldwide US$ figure unavailable

"*Angel* carries knockout power. A story of retribution set against the troubles in Northern Ireland which are kept way in the background, it's an impressive pic debut for director-scriptor Neil Jordan." Variety staff, *Variety*

Angel has a lot to answer for. This is the film that launched both Neil Jordan and Stephen Rea (with his hound-dog expressions). Without this picture we would have been spared so many poor and overrated movies (see further on for various offerings from Mr. Jordan).

No cliché is left untapped as we travel through "Oirland" trying to find a reason behind the madness of violence (no explanation given as to the madness of funding this film though). From religion to mysticism, and including lots of doleful looks and annoying saxophone music, the film tries to capture the soul of the country. But actually, this is perhaps one of the most pretentious movies ever to come out of Ireland.

Brimming with pseudo-intellectualism and a belief that if you don't actually tell the audience anything then they will convince themselves that something is actually happening, this really is a film with delusions of mediocrity. A great example of style over content – were, indeed, the picture to have any style, I challenge you to watch this beside *The Commitments* (1991) (or even *I Went Down* (1997)) and recognize the same country. A lot of the problem seems to be that the director has not cottoned on to the fact that the Northern Irish accent is flat and dull, and can be very boring unless it's telling a joke or screaming at people with different religious views while blowing their heads off. If you do endure this drab film listen out for the completely monotone "you move me" line, which is unintentionally hilarious.

Still … without *Angel* this book would probably have been *50 Movies to Avoid*.

Angela's Ashes

An adaptation of Frank McCourt's bestseller, *Angela's Ashes* tells the story of Frankie's childhood and adolescence in Ireland during the 1930s and 40s, coping with horrific poverty and an alcoholic father.

Director	Alan Parker
Writers	Alan Parker, Laura Jones (from the book by Frank McCourt)
Starring	Emily Watson
	Robert Carlyle
Released	1999
Awards	IFTA Awards for Best Feature Film and Best Craft Achievement. Nominated for Best Original Score at the Oscars. Nominated for three BAFTAs: Best Production Design, Best Cinematography, Best Leading Actress (Emily Watson)
Box office	$15,138,660 (Worldwide)

"A fine muckrake in the Dickensian tradition, perhaps from *Angela's Ashes* will rise a phoenix of renewed compassion and caring. For Frank's sake." Michael S. Goldberger, *Movie Reviews UK*

A classic and much-loved book that captures the very essence of the human spirit, two of the most talented film actors, amazing sets and genuine settings, not to mention possibly the greatest living movie director ... what could possibly go wrong?

In a word: self-indulgence. Rather than concentrating on the great personal story, Parker opts to create his own lasting masterpiece, and misfires completely. Scene after scene of the boys running in the rain, and visions of Emily Watson pushing the ramshackle pram again up cobbled streets, do get irritating. The overbearing and nullifying John Williams soundtrack adds to the general gut feeling of "get on with it".

This is a strange inclusion for the book because the film was not what could be called lauded (indeed it was only nominated for one Oscar – curiously for the annoying music, but that's the American Academy for you). But it is overrated simply because it was not trashed as much as it should have been. Because of the director and the source material, the media and most cinemagoers were fairly charitable toward it.

And that, to me, is a mistake (allowing Mr. Parker to then go on and make the ludicrous *The Life of David Gale* (2003)). People should have been brave enough to stand up and be counted, telling it as it was – ie. that *Angela's Ashes* was a folly. None of the joie de vivre from the novel was really communicated, and the extremely talented cast were sadly underused (sweeping shots taking precedence over any idea of substance).

The result is a depressing and shallow journey. The poster should have read: "If you loved the book, then stay away!"

The Aviator

The story of the early days of the tortured genius Howard Hughes, and his influence on the movie and aviation industries.

Director	Martin Scorsese
Writer	John Logan
Starring	Leonardo DiCaprio
	Cate Blanchett
	Kate Beckinsale
	John C. Reilly
Released	2004
Awards	Five Oscars, and nominated for six more. Four BAFTAS including, Best Film, nominated for 10 more. Three Golden Globes, including Best Motion Picture and Best Actor, nominated for three more. And so on, and on…
Box office	$173,608,827 (Worldwide)
Tagline	Some men dream the future. He built it.

"*The Aviator* is imposing, spectacular, and hard to get off the ground. But when it takes off, it soars." Nev Pierce, BBCi

Martin Scorsese should pay more attention to the career of Mohammed Ali. The boxing legend stayed in the ring far too long. Not only did this upset his millions of fans who squirmed to see him well past his best, but it also caused the great man to suffer severe brain damage. Let's hope the same doesn't happen to "Marty" – the man who gave us *Mean Streets* (1973), *Taxi Driver* (1976), *Goodfellas* (1990), *The King of Comedy* (1983) … the list could go on forever (let's not forget the very underrated *After Hours* (1985)). But after watching *The Aviator*, I narrowly escaped damage myself (two hours of hitting your head against the wall trying to get the film out of your memory does that!).

Lauded by press and those toadying awards organizations, it has to be asked if the same film would have received a third of the praise had Mr. M. Nobody been the director. How can you mess up with a central figure such as Howard Hughes? The cinematic potential is unlimited.

But instead we get a shallow and linear tale that lacks focus or pizzazz. For nearly three bum-numbing hours we are force-fed a film that is undoubtedly on autopilot. This is not helped by casting the less than one-dimensional pretty boy DiCaprio in the lead (when he starts to sprout facial hair it is hard not to think of children trying to look grown up). But it still has to be remembered that the major blame must go to Scorsese.

This is a film that is not about anything – it doesn't try to tell us anything, discuss any themes or even vaguely entertain us. Some psycho-babble about his mother washing him is replayed in a vain attempt to explain Hughes's obsessions, but you come out of the movie as ill-informed about the man behind the legend as you went in. Watch out Marty, the fans won't always cover for you.

Bad Education

Two boys suffer abuse, both mental and physical, at a Catholic school in Franco's Spain. The damaging repercussions spread throughout their lives.

Director	Pedro Almodóvar
Writer	Pedro Almodóvar
Starring	Gael García Bernal
	Fele Martínez
	Daniel Giménez Cacho
Released	2004
Awards	Won Best Director at Italian National Syndicate of Film Journalists, and three Glitter Awards, including Best Picture and Best Actor Nominated for a César, several European Film Awards, a BAFTA and about a million other awards you never heard of.
Box office	Worldwide US$ figure unavailable

"Pedro Almodóvar has done it again. His new movie is a dizzying and rapturous noir melodrama, a little like Hitchcock's *Vertigo* with layers of confusion and contradiction." Peter Bradshaw, *Guardian*

Everyone has a bad day at the office. Robbie Williams recently offered an audience a free concert because he felt he had underperformed. The late, great, George Best had a few stinkers on the football field (although, granted, they may have been self-induced – and he wouldn't have remembered them anyway). So why can't film critics admit that Almodóvar underperformed with *Bad Education*? Maybe it's because of the edgy themes, or they simply don't want to be seen as homophobic (imagine being scared of your own home), but whatever it is no one had the nerve to stand up and say that this film about little boys being sexually abused wasn't very good.

The Spanish director can be excused a few blunders in his life after all the pleasure he's given us. And there can be many reasons why *Bad Education* is so flawed – perhaps Almodóvar was too close to the story? Or it could just be that he can't make good films about men (all his greatest moments are female-centric pictures – *All About My Mother* (1999), *Volver* (2006), *Woman on the Verge of a Nervous Breakdown* (1988)). Whatever it was, the truth is that when this film isn't unpleasant it's just dull and predictable.

If there's a lesson here for critics it's don't be afraid to criticize a film just because you like the rest of the director's work. Just because you love Coke doesn't mean that you had to enjoy Tab!

Bad Lieutenant

A corrupt drug-addicted policeman seeks redemption after encountering a nun who instantly forgives the monster who rapes her.

Director	Abel Ferrara
Writers	Abel Ferrara, Victor Argo, Paul Calderon, Zoë Lund, Mary Kane
Starring	Harvey Keitel
	Victor Argo
	Paul Calderone
Released	1992
Awards	International Fantasy Film Award for Best Actor, nominated for Best Film. Independent Spirit Award for Best Male Lead and nominated for Best Director and Best Feature.
Box office	Worldwide US$ figure unavailable
Tagline	Gambler…Thief…Junkie…Killer…Cop

"The Lieutenant is like a rogue, self-flagellating saint drawing himself closer to God through willful defiance – a tormented, bedeviled man engaged in unholy communion." Hal Hinson, *Washington Post*

Beautiful, bleak, harrowing … you hear this again and again about *Bad Lieutenant*. Don't believe a word. It's just another basic thrown-together mishmash of graphic scenes and ambivalent themes that Ferrara uses to pull the wool over audiences' eyes. The director grossly uses shock tactics to get attention, and then coats a light sheen over his work to leave you desperately searching for the message that you think should be there.

Don't waste your time – there's nothing under the surface. This is a film for people who want to see nuns raped and a dirty old man masturbating over teenagers. Just because Harvey Keitel is in it doesn't mean that it's not a run-of-the mill video nasty.

The film has been lauded as an exploration of Catholic themes and an investigation into the frailty of mankind. But what you really get is a fairly tawdry (and extremely bland) film that actually bores more than disgusts. Keitel grunts his way through the episodic mess without ever offering clues to the protagonist's character arc, or even a sense of what the hell is going on.

There's nothing wrong with degradation (in its own place), and people are free to enjoy watching whatever they want (within certain legal guidelines … unless you're a rock star). But to then dress it as art, and try to pretend there's an inner meaning, is just duplicitous in the extreme.

Bad Lieutenant is neither art nor smart – get off on it if you will, but don't look for a deeper message (or even entertainment).

Batman

Billionaire playboy Bruce Wayne takes on the cape of the Dark Knight to protect a Gotham City from the evil power of The Joker.

Director	Tim Burton
Writers	Bob Kane, Sam Hamm, Warren Skaaren
Starring	Michael Keaton
	Jack Nicholson
	Kim Basinger
Released	1989
Awards	Oscar for Best Art Direction-Set Direction, BMI Film Music Award, Brit for Best Soundtrack, two People's Choice Awards. Nominated for several BAFTAs, a Golden Globe and two Grammys.
Box office	$413,200,000 (Worldwide)

"*Batman* is a hugely influential movie with literally towering design, mordant wit, and a hall-of-fame performance by Jack Nicholson." Peter Canavese, *Groucho Reviews*

There is so much garbage written about Batman – his history, the darker side of his story, blah blah blah. And sadly Tim Burton fell for it. A comic is a comic is a comic – not a bloody "graphic novel" or the like (sorry to disappoint the throngs of young men still living with their mothers and slowly going blind in front of their computers). It's not supposed to be taken too seriously – there's no coincidence that comedians are referred to as "comics".

Amid a wave of euphoria about the new "darker" Batman character it was deemed something akin to heresy-meets-treason to actually say that you liked Adam West in the TV series. Instead we had to all pretend that this was the real deal – a po-faced Michael Keaton morosely going about his business (sadly the end of Keaton's career really, which started so promisingly with *Johnny Dangerously* (1984) and *Night Shift* (1982)).

So let's put a few things straight: The Gotham set wasn't fantastic – it was a couple of cardboard backdrops that are used again and again. This movie actually looks really cheap and the production design lacks any imagination or flair. Jack Nicholson faxed in his performance as The Joker – this is no inspired routine, it's a basic rehash of every other role he has ever done (you almost hear him screaming "here's Johnny").

The recent *Batman Begins* (2005) shows how to make a more serious take on the fragility of the human psyche and still show great action and keep a story going. *Batman* failed in every department. Don't listen to the perennial bachelors, if you want to have a bit of fun with someone dressing as a bat then put George Clooney in the lead role and Alicia Silverstone in a school uniform.

The Beach

A young American backpacker discovers the illusive "perfect beach" in Thailand, but his idea of heaven soon descends into hell.

Director	Danny Boyle
Writer	John Hodge (from the book by Alex Garland)
Starring	Leonardo DiCaprio
	Tilda Swinton
	Virginie Ledoyen
	Robert Carlyle
Released	2000
Awards	Nominated for a Golden Berlin Bear, a Brit, a Golden Trailer Award (for Best Voice Over), a Teen Choice and best of all, a Razzie for Worst Actor (Leonardo DiCaprio).
Box office	$143,278,599 (Worldwide)
Tagline	Innocence never lasts forever.

"… this is a pacy youth-generation thriller with a rollicking soundtrack and a sharp millennial message about how travel does not broaden dangerously narrow minds." (uncredited) Britmovie.co.uk

So many people loved the book that they just convinced themselves to love the film too. Having happily escaped the source novel, I was able to watch the film with unbiased eyes. And what a horribly dull and unconvincing film it is.

Perhaps the main problem is why he wanted to go to an unremarkable stretch of sand with a bunch of annoying middle-class twits in tie-dye anyway. I have to say the previous beach looked much better to me – Singha beer served to the beach lounger, and Virginie Ledoyen smiling over at you. Paradise? The idiot already had it and just didn't realize it.

What's worse, when he gets there he shags Tilda Swinton. Urgh! I wasn't expecting this to be a horror movie. Haven't you seen *Orlando* Leo? She's really a bloke. But at least that scene wasn't quite as dreadful as little Leonardo and the very sexy Ledoyen getting it on in the water. Possibly one of the worst love scenes in cinematic history.

But maybe it was supposed to be a comedy. The scenes where DiCaprio goes la-la are just so preposterous that they must have been intentional. And we get Robert Carlyle jumping up and down as a mad Scotsman (you're much better than that Bobby).

To this day, I still have no idea what *The Beach* was trying to say, or trying to do. You feel that there must have been a point to it, other than don't go on holidays with effeminate and rather dull Americans, but none ever springs to mind.

Bean

Our bungling hero is sent to the US to unveil *Whistler's Mother* in an LA Gallery.

Director	Mel Smith
Writers	Rowan Atkinson, Richard Curtis, Robin Driscoll
Starring	Rowan Atkinson
	Peter MacNicol
	Sir John Mills
	Pamela Reed
Released	1997
Awards	Two awards in Germany: a Bogey award in Platinum and Golden Screen award
Box office	$232,000,000 (Worldwide)
Tagline	One Man. One Masterpiece. One Very Big Mistake.

"His name is Bean, and he's already a legume in his own lifetime." Desson Howe, *Washington Post*

"The surprise is that Rowan Atkinson, who can be wearisome, stays funny throughout his crazy new comedy, spritzing the inane with refreshing intelligence." Peter Stack, *San Francisco Chronicle*

God I hate Bean. Two minutes of the television show just sends me in apoplexy. He's utterly annoying, the humour is lowest common denominator and most of the "jokes" are stolen from elsewhere. So those nice people at Working Title decided that we needed a movie – 90 whole minutes with the "lovable buffoon". Great. And worse, it was a hit. The lowest common denominator worked and the movie stormed the box office all over the world (the East Europeans were especially keen – you'd have thought they had suffered enough what with Communism and now *Eurovision*).

I have nothing but respect for a man who can make people laugh. But Rowan Atkinson … purleeese. His "rubbery" face and the obvious double-takes are irritating in the extreme. He also manages to make this horrible noise throughout his portrayal of Bean, something akin to a grunt really. The comedy, for what it is, is cheap and predictable. There's only so many times you can laugh at an idiot fall over or walk into something – come on, this character is obviously mentally retarded. There, I hope that's wiped the smirk off your faces.

The movie itself has no plot except for sending Bean to America. There is also no character for us to get to know. The audience don't laugh with Bean (well, I definitely don't), they cruelly laugh at him.

So, if you have any depth of compassion in your soul, avoid Bean – honestly, it's for the best all round.

A Beautiful Mind

John Nash is a brilliant mathematician, but his complex work and undercover CIA details lead to bouts of depression and even schizophrenia.

Director	Ron Howard
Writer	Akiva Goldsman (from the book by Sylvia Nasar)
Starring	Russell Crowe
	Ed Harris
	Jennifer Connelly
	Christopher Plummer
	Paul Bettany
Released	2001
Awards	Four Oscars including Best Picture and Director, nominated for four more. Two BAFTAs for Jennifer Connelly and Russell Crowe, nominated for three more. Another 25 wins and 39 nominations.
Box office	$312,100,000 (Worldwide)
Tagline	It is only in the mysterious equation of love that any logical reasons can be found.

"*A Beautiful Mind* is a greatly ambitious undertaking, but from the commercial point of view quite insane. The movie is ridiculously fragile: it's like a Fabergé egg, and even a twitch of foreknowledge will destroy the magic of the movie utterly. That is why I will say no more. Anything else, and we're beyond journalism and into desecration." Stephen Hunter, *Washington Post*

What the hell is this all about? Why would we be interested in some mad maths genius stumbling around jotting numbers on a blackboard? You can see nutters outside every train station, mumbling away into their cans of lager. You don't need to pay to watch them on the big screen. Granted, there is a nice twist (turn the page now if you don't know it, and are still thinking that some day you might waste your time on this) – ie. that the Paul Bettany character doesn't exist. But that's about it, and it's certainly no *Sixth Sense* reveal.

So how can such a dull load of old nonsense win lots of Oscars (and why am I asking so many rhetorical questions in this section? Maybe I'm losing it like poor old John Nash?). Well there's some hokum thrown in about Nash working for the CIA (all very trendy around this time with *Confessions of a Dangerous Mind* (2002) out then too), which apparently gives the film depth and commerciality. And the old buffers at the American Academy all fondly remember *Happy Days,* so Richie Cunningham (aka Ron Howard) is always going to be odds-on favourite for a prize if he is involved in a movie. In fact Pottsie could probably pick up a gong, except that he's been busy directing *Beverly Hills 90210, Lizzie McGuire* and re-launches of *The Love Boat* (I kid you not).

But the biggest mystery of all is how Jennifer Connelly managed to steal a BAFTA award for her performance. Let's be honest – you go for Connelly if you don't have enough money for Demi Moore. You can count on her to give you glassy, far-away stares and a nice dress hangs on her OK. But there's nothing else. Don't look for any hidden depth, she ain't got none! Never mind Paul Bettany, I was convinced that Jennifer Connelly didn't exist in this film.

Beetlejuice

A recently deceased couple want to scare away the new inhabitants of their home, and so employ the services of a "bio-exorcist".

Director	Tim Burton
Writers	Michael McDowell, Warren Skaaren, Larry Wilson
Starring	Alec Baldwin
	Geena Davis
	Michael Keaton
	Winona Ryder
Released	1988
Awards	An Oscar for Best Makeup, A BMI Film Music Award, Best Actor (Michael Keaton) at National Society of Film Critics Awards, USA. Nominated for two BAFTAs.
Box office	Worldwide US$ figure unavailable
Tagline	The Name In Laughter From The Hereafter.

"*Beetlejuice* is an extraspectral experience, a wonderfully wacko look at the hereafter's relationship with the here and now. It's a cartoon view of the afterlife landscape, where the living haunt the dead and death's no escape from life's little irritants – like waiting rooms and elevator music." Rita Kempley, *Washington Post*

What is it about Tim Burton and Michael Keaton? Great director, fabulous actor, but when they get together it's murder (as they say at the start of *Hart to Hart*).

Beetlejuice was lauded as original, fun, spiky and charming – why? There is something essentially boring about someone trying self-consciously to be zany and wacky. It is usually forgiven in teenagers trying desperately to impress, but I spent hard-earned money on the admission fee for this feat of adolescent showing-off.

Let's shoot from the hip here – the film is not original: Dennis Potter had been using the lip-synching sequences ten years before and *The Ghost and Mrs. Muir* (1947) was much more proficient at summoning interesting characters from the dead. Not only is Michael Keaton actually not the lead character, he is in the film for a very short period. And say it loud – he's very annoying! This is not some manic comic performance, it's an ill-prepared improvisation that substitutes obtuse and obvious statements for genuinely inspired humour.

Tedious as Keaton's interspersions are, without them we are left with Alec Baldwin and Geena Davis being dull. Even Winona Ryder failed to steal any scenes. There is none of the magic of *Edward Scissorhands* (1990) or the charm of *Ed Wood* (1994), and it never gets close to the anarchy of *Pee-wee's Big Adventure* (1985). So if anyone tells you that they're a fan of Burton and they love *Beetlejuice*, take it with a big pinch of salt.

Belle de Jour

While unable to become intimate with the doctor husband who she loves, a bored housewife takes up the oldest profession in the world to while away her afternoons.

Director	Luis Buñuel
Writers	Luis Buñuel, Jean-Claude Carrière (from the book by Joseph Kessel)
Starring	Catherine Deneuve
	Jean Sorel
	Michel Piccoli
Released	1967
Awards	One BAFTA for Catherine Deneuve, Best Film at the French Syndicate of Cinema Critics, Best European Film at the Bodil Awards, and two awards at the Venice Film Festival.
Box office	No figures available

"It is possibly the best-known erotic film of modern times, perhaps the best. That's because it understands eroticism from the inside-out – understands how it exists not in sweat and skin, but in the imagination." Roger Ebert, *Chicago Sun-Times*

You gotta hand it to *Belle de Jour*. It's gotten away with it for so long, I almost don't want to be the one to debunk the myth. The film is seen as Buñuel's "masterpiece" – exploring sexuality and the human psyche. Yeah, right. What actually has happened is that some dirty old man has put his wet dreams onto celluloid – called it art rather than porn – and everyone's bought it. If this was in English everyone would just presume that it was directed by Michael Winner.

Deneuve is a beautiful bored housewife who, deep, deep down, only really wants to have sex – the harder the better. A bit of rape does her no harm at all either. How *Belle de Jour* can be considered anything more than a misogynist flight of fancy is beyond me. It's not an exploration of sensuality; it's a pretty sordid skin flick that uses art as an excuse for masturbation. When the Spanish director (who, no doubt, had very hairy palms) brings you Deneuve's character's fantasies, he's really conveying his own.

I have nothing against a bit of titillation. But *Belle de Jour* is particularly nasty because it uses the cloak of arty-fartyness and, more worryingly, portrays quite violent and dangerous fantasies that could lead to people being hurt. The basic premise is that all women are really "mad for it" – if you're not getting what you want just slap her around a bit (she loves it really). The luvvies that laud this tawdry mess (and Martin Scorsese, shame on him, actively campaigned to have the file re-released on DVD) are the same that shouted down Gaspar Noé's *Irréversible* (2002). *Belle de Jour* is not just a bad film, it is a dangerous one.

Billy Elliot

A young boy from a tough mining town that is in the middle of a vicious and divisive strike, dreams of becoming a ballet dancer against the wishes of his family.

Director	Stephen Daldry
Writer	Lee Hall
Starring	Jamie Bell
	Jean Heywood
	Gary Lewis
	Julie Walters
Released	2000
Awards	Three BAFTAs, and nominated for 10 more. Also won three Empire awards, two Evening Standard awards etc. etc. Nominated for three Oscars, two Golden Globes etc., etc.
Box office	$98,749,911 (Worldwide)
Tagline	Inside every one of us is a special talent waiting to come out. The trick is finding it.

"Watch your back, Haley Joel Osment: Bell explodes onscreen in a performance that cuts to the heart without sham tear-jerking. When Billy confronts his father not with words or fists but with a dance that gives form and grace to his anger, the result is one of the most powerful scenes of the movie year. Look for Billy to blast off." Peter Travers, *Rolling Stone*

Absolute rubbish. This is a film that is badly conceived (cliché following cliché), badly written, badly directed, and suffers from some of the worst acting known to man (only the ever-reliable Julie Walters gets away unscathed). Even for sloppy sentimental Sunday night television *Billy Elliot* is poor, so how on earth did it become so popular and respected?

The film has been fêted for its integrity, which is startling as it is contrived and feels fake throughout (I refer especially to the supposedly violent scenes that are up there with *West Side Story*'s opening for conveying counterfeit aggression). There's no gritty realism here (supposedly contrasted with the beauty of the dancing – more about that in a minute). This is how middle-class film people believe working-class northerners live and behave. It's all as quaint and cosy as a bread advert.

And as for Ballet Bill himself … I'm sorry, did I miss something? He's irksome, and frankly I wouldn't have let him go to dance lessons either. The whole irony is that many would agreed with his Dad – maybe ballet dancing is a little bit gay, and with the town starving surely there are much more important things for him to be doing (couldn't he find a paper round?).

My other major bugbear with *Billy Elliot* is that Billy can't even dance. He's rubbish. The dance scenes are laughably bad, with the annoying little toe-rag doing little more than jumping and stomping around the place (Kathy Bates would be more graceful and agile). Send him down the mines, or up chimneys – just keep him away from me.

Bird

The life and times of the great jazzman, Charlie (Bird) Parker.

Director	Clint Eastwood
Writer	Jack N. Green
Starring	Forest Whitaker
	Diane Venora
	Michael Zelniker
Released	1988
Awards	Oscar for Best Sound, the Technical Grand Prize and Best Actor at Cannes, and a Golden Globe for Best Director. Nominated for two BAFTAs, a César and two more Golden Globe.
Box office	Worldwide US$ figure unavailable
Tagline	"There are no second acts in American lives." – F. Scott Fitzgerald

"… the image of the great young actor Forest Whitaker standing dead still on the bandstand, with only his fingers moving over the buttons of his horn, is hauntingly definitive, yet somehow shadowy and enigmatic, like a figure drawn in smoke." Hal Hinson, *Washington Post*

It is hard to recall someone who has had more influence over film in the last 50 years than Clint Eastwood. From his pitch perfect performances as an actor, in many cases making it respectable to like commercial pictures, to his stunning directorial efforts, Clint is a man among men in the movie industry. But let's be honest, old gravelly voice: this one was just for you wasn't it?

We know he loves jazz, and is obviously a Parker fan. But *Bird* sadly has no real purpose or direction. The thing that people forget with biopics is that they still need a story, and a point – someone has to want something, and someone has to try to stop them. All we get here is a fat jazzman taking too many drugs and dying young (sorry if that counts as a spoiler – but come on, if you didn't know he was dead you wouldn't want to see the film in the first place).

The other problem is that the film never actually illustrates to us why Charlie Parker was a genius. It's hard for us mere mortals to understand what made him different to your average saxophonist who constantly rehashes "Take Five" in the subway. Without discovering what elevated Parker above the rest, the film is useless. It also means that we don't care about Parker being a junkie – we don't understand his gift so don't really care if he misuses it.

A bit like sex, watching *Bird* is nowhere near the experience it must have been to hear the musician in his prime. A decent enough performance from Forest Whitaker (an unlikely leading man) makes the film slightly bearable, but it's definitely not the masterpiece that people say it is.

Blair Witch Project

Three student filmmakers travel to the woods to shoot a documentary about a local myth, the Blair Witch – a year later their footage is found.

Directors	Daniel Myrick, Eduardo Sanchez
Writers	Daniel Myrick, Eduardo Sanchez
Starring	Heather Donahue
	Joshua Leonard
	Michael Williams
Released	1999
Awards	Two Golden Trailers, a Foreign Film prize at Cannes, and an Independent Spirit Award, as well as two Razzies, one for Heather, one for the film. Nominated for a number of awards including three Blockbuster Entertainment Awards and a Bram Stoker award.
Box office	$240,500,000 (Worldwide)
Tagline	Everything you've heard is true.

"*Blair Witch Project* is probably the closest thing I've seen cinematically to capture those childhood feelings of spooky bogeymen in the dark." Robert A. Fulkerson, *Manly Men's Movie Reviews*

Powered by hype, *Blair Witch Project* scared the pants off the moviegoers at the end of the last century. And it just goes to show, you can sell a dog if you tell people long enough it's a thoroughbred horse. But in the cold light of day it has to be said: *Blair Witch Project* is simply not very scary.

And that's all you really need to know. The film is cynical to the extreme, managing to find excuses for poor production and slack story by simply passing it off as a student project. There's many a stroke of genius in the ideas behind *Blair Witch Project*, and certainly in the marketing, but the film itself is pretty poor.

The Exorcist is scary, *The Shining* is scary, *Blair Witch Project* is dull. The scary part of the whole exercise is the mass hysteria the marketing created. Watch it again now and you really won't understand what all the fuss is about. The performances are so bad that you really hope they do meet their maker, and as painfully as possible. The camerawork isn't bewitching, it's just jerky and distracting. And no one actually knows what the whole thing is about.

So the end product is a mildly diverting historical artefact that in years to come will be as confounding to our successors in this green world as the penny farthing is to us. The greatest horror of *Blair Witch Project* is the amount of even cheaper, and even less scary, imitations that saturated the market in the aftermath.

Not quite as bad as the woeful sequel (a real horror in a different way), *Blair Witch Project* is a bit like someone jumping out in front of you and shouting "boo!" It's cheap, unimaginative, the first time it might give you a jump. But after that you're expecting the "shock" and can't work out why the perpetrator is still doing it again and again.

The Bourne Supremacy

After lying low and trying to forget what he can't really remember, ex-CIA man Bourne is thrown back into the melee of violence and espionage.

Director	Paul Greengrass
Writer	Tony Gilroy (from the book by Robert Ludlum)
Starring	Matt Damon
	Franka Potente
	Brian Cox
	Julia Stiles
Released	2004
Awards	Won 5 awards including two Empire Awards for Best Film and Actor. Nominated for 17 others.
Box office	$272,549,130
Tagline	They should have left him alone.

"The multi-talented Matt Damon returns for this stylish follow-up to *The Bourne Identity*." Louisa McLennan, Times Online

"This is among the most frantic pictures ever made; the camera is endlessly restless, the editing is frenetic, with images bordering on the subliminal..." Philip French, *Observer*

If the first damp squib was not bad enough, the powers that be decided that the world was licking its lips in anticipation of a sequel. All rather strange as the original picture revolved around the question of who the protagonist is, a conundrum that is solved at the end of the film. So what can a sequel really offer except for a run-of-the-mill espionage thriller?

The answer is, very little. Matt Damon is not the most charismatic of actors anyway, and the character was never really fleshed out into an interesting role.

But the "masterstroke" from the producers was to bring in British director Paul Greengrass (whose previous work had mostly been docu-drama, including the brilliant *Bloody Sunday*). Greengrass's directing style in this film can be described in one line: swing the camera around again and again. *The Bourne Supremacy* is the cinematic equivalent of a ride on a waltzer at those old fashioned funfairs. I challenge you to sit through the picture and not come out dizzy.

It's not just in the action scenes, which are tame and tiresome to say the least – Greengrass has the camera spinning, or jumping up and down at all times, during the most bizarre of moments. I usually like movies that keep you on the edge of your seat – but not when it's because you're about to vomit.

Still, take away the whirling dervish of a camera and there's not much left to remember – dodgy plot, bad performances, stilted dialogue and a really cold look (which manages to make Julia Stiles seem unattractive). In fact, everything an action movie shouldn't have (hence the "experts" lauding it as an "intelligent action thriller" … intelligent obviously meaning shit in their language).

More thrills to be had on a wet Wednesday in Wakefield, and the only spills to expect is when you finally puke your popcorn onto your lap.

Brazil

In a bizarre futuristic society, a civil servant tries to right an administrative error which has led to the wrong man being arrested.

Director	Terry Gilliam
Writers	Terry Gilliam, Tom Stoppard, Charles McKeown
Starring	Jonathan Pryce
	Robert De Niro
	Katherine Helmond
Released	1985
Awards	Two BAFTAs, three Los Angeles Film Critics Association Awards, two Boston Society of Film Critics Awards. Nominated for two Oscars and a Hugo.
Box office	Worldwide US$ figure unavailable
Tagline	It's only a state of mind.

"Terry Gilliam's masterpiece so far would be *Brazil* since it perfectly shoots at what he wants and gets right on target. Besides, it's just so damn cool." Ted Prigge, Britmovie.co.uk

OK, if you think it's that easy – you write a short synopsis of *Brazil*. The whole thing is baffling. There's something about heating engineers and air ducts, and some woman who keeps on appearing in Jonathan Pryce's dreams (and then in his reality … if, indeed, you could call this reality). But all in all it's really just Terry Gilliam messing us around, isn't it?

Yes there is some visual flair on show, but you would expect that from the ex-Python anyway. But the film as a whole is simply very boring. I don't mind being baffled or bamboozled by a movie, God knows *The Big Sleep* (1946) asked a lot more questions than it answered. But I really hate to be bored stupid by a film (I fell asleep the first two times I tried to watch *Brazil*).

And the visuals aren't even very original. The adjective always used is "Orwellian," that's because Gilliam stole any inspiration he had from *Nineteen Eighty-Four* (1984). It's almost his own private joke at the book's expense. And, to be honest, I really don't want to spend nearly three hours watching someone else's private joke Terry. People will espouse the dream sequences, and the "hilarious" dialogue. Trust me – stay away. Unless you need a really good night's kip that is. There's not even any samba dancing in it.

Broken Flowers

An aging Lothario receives a note telling him that he might have a son looking for him, which inspires him to travel the country tracking down old girlfriends.

Director	Jim Jarmusch
Writer	Jim Jarmusch (inspired by an idea by Bill Raden and Sara Driver)
Starring	Bill Murray
	Julie Delpy
	Heather Alicia Simms
Released	2005
Awards	Grand Prize at Cannes, and nominated for a Golden Palm. Two other wins and nine other nominations.
Box office	Worldwide US$ figure unavailable
Tagline	Sometimes life brings some strange surprises.

"Jim Jarmusch's new film is a lugubrious, lenient, sweetly acted comedy about male middle-age, and it has been Jarmusch's greatest box office success so far, arguably his first real box office success." Peter Bradshaw, *Guardian*

OK, we've got Bill Murray. So we throw in quite a lot of *Lost in Translation* (2003) and add a fair portion of *The Life Aquatic with Steve Zissou* (2004) … what could possibly go wrong?

Shame on you Jim Jarmusch – the man who gave us *Ghost Dog* (1997), *Dead Man* (1995) and *Mystery Train* (1989). This is lazy, lazy film making. And shame too on all the critics who lazily just decided that it's Jarmusch and Murray, so it must be good. For God's sake keep your eyes and your brains open: you're public servants you know.

It's not even that *Broken Flowers* is bad. It's just boring. "Broken Records" might have been a better title as the story goes around again and again until you don't really care any more.

That's perhaps the most annoying thing about the whole movie: it starts so well. We're all waiting for it to develop. There's kookiness, in-jokes, some great visual flair (it is worth watching the first thirty minutes just to witness the segment with Lolita). But the damned movie never builds on the initial promise. Instead he visits another "wacky" ex-girlfriend, and another; with no progression and by the end you actually forget the point of the story completely.

It's not helped by Murray faxing in his performance (he and Jack Nicholson must have huge phone bills these days). We'd forgotten how lazy he had got (let's be honest, he seems much happier just voicing Garfield now) thanks to *Lost in Translation* (and he didn't want to do that – apparently Sofia Coppola had to chase him for a year before he would even return a call). But Jim Jarmusch should know better. He's proven what an individualistic director he is, so why would he have settled with this odd hybrid?

I really feel sorry for the excellent female cast that try their level best around Murray, especially the excellent Jessica Lange. But don't let the lazy critics blind you just because they're as indolent as Murray. There's nothing fresh about these flowers.

Calendar Girls

A group of Women's Institute ladies decide to pose nude for a calendar to raise money for charity, much to the distaste of other members and the local "respectable" community.

Director	Nigel Cole
Writers	Tim Firth, Juliette Towhidi
Starring	Helen Mirren
	Julie Walters
	John Alderton
Released	2003
Awards	Two awards, one of them a British Comedy Award, and 10 nominations including a Golden Globe.
Box office	Worldwide US$ figure unavailable.
Tagline	They dropped everything for a good cause.

"Such is our craving for homegrown success that any half-decent British movie released since 1997 has immediately been dubbed the next *Full Monty*. For once, though, *Calendar Girls* … lives up to that description." Neil Smith, BBCi

This is a film that really perplexes me. I saw a screening very early on and confidently predicted that the flick would be a huge flop. It's smug, prissy, derivative, old-fashioned, and doesn't know where to end. So who could like it?

Suddenly, what should be a Sunday afternoon background to a good snooze is being proclaimed from the hilltops. It's almost as if the next *Citizen Kane* had been discovered. Granted, a very impressive press campaign meant the film was everywhere. I can see why it did OK at the box office, with many simply convinced that this is the movie for them (especially those wrinkly old people that only go to one film a year). But surely no one, after having to sit through this, would come out saying that it was any good – would they?

Well let's put the record straight. *Calendar Girls* is not "delightful", and it certainly isn't worthy to tie the shoe-laces (or close the Velcro) of *The Full Monty*. The story is twee, predictable and we know the ending. I don't want to see a pack of old birds getting their floppy bits out, so it's neither naughty or raunchy, it's just plain embarrassing. And the film gets no brownie points for cynically throwing in a cancer patient. I know that this was part of the true story, and the calendar raised money for leukaemia research, but the style (if you can call it that) in the movie was mawkish and almost using this as an excuse for the silliness later (although at least John Alderton is the one watchable performance).

And worst of all, the girls finally get their calendar and it's a huge success. "Hurrah," says I, "time for the pub." Oh no, the cruel, cruel film makers make you sit through another 20 minutes of sublime garbage. The girls go to America, one of their sons goes missing … blah, blah, blah. What's the point? Let us out! If there were some cinematic equivalent of the war crimes trials then the makers of *Calendar Girls* would surely be convicted.

Chariots of Fire

Two young British runners compete against each other, and against the world, to run in the 1924 Olympics

Director	Hugh Hudson
Writer	Colin Welland
Starring	Nicholas Farrell
	Nigel Havers
	Ian Charleson
	Ben Cross
Released	1981
Awards	Four Oscars including Best Picture and Best Screenplay, and two nominations. Three BAFTAs, including Best Film, and eight nominations. Two prizes at Cannes, a Golden Globe … blah … blah
Box office	Worldwide US$ figure unavailable
Tagline	Two men chasing dreams of glory!

"… with music by the Greek composer Vangelis Papathanassiou. His compositions for *Chariots of Fire* are as evocative, and as suited to the material, as the different but also perfectly matched scores of such films as *The Third Man* and *Zorba the Greek*." Roger Ebert, *Chicago Sun-Times*

"The British are coming," proclaimed the writer of *Chariots of Fire*, the late Colin Welland, at the Oscars. They obviously ran out of petrol if this rather tame offering is anything to go by.

I can see why the original story would have attracted the producers – it has the excitement of sport, all the visual spectacle of a period drama, plus very universal themes and two interesting characters.

If only they hadn't gone to mad Greek Vangelis for the soundtrack. Without the horrible electronic tunes, which sounded like they were composed by Rolf Harris on his Stylophone, this could have been a passable movie (although still not the multi-Oscar winner it turned out to be). The backing music burns its way into your brains (come on, admit it, you're humming de-da-de-da da, da as you're reading) and immediately tells you to go to sleep.

So we've got a terrible soundtrack – what else can we add to really annoy the audience? How about using slow motion all the time, so that Vangelis's monotonous passages seem neverending? There's probably only about 40 minutes of real footage in *Chariots of Fire*, but it's shown again and again in slow-mo to drag out the film.

I feel unpatriotic to mention it, but thankfully the British never actually made it (or maybe they're in slow motion, so are still on their way).

The Cider House Rules

Having never been chosen for adoption Homer has always lived in the orphanage, growing up to be assistant to the director of the institute. But now he wants to break the ties and stand up on his own two feet.

Director	Lasse Hallström
Writer	John Irving (from his own book)
Starring	Tobey Maguire
	Charlize Theron
	Delroy Lindo
	Paul Rudd
Released	1999
Awards	Two Oscars,one for the screenplay, one for Michael Caine, and five nominations. Two other wins for the screenplay, one for Erykah Badu as Best Supporting Actress, and a host of nominations, including five for Michael Caine.
Box office	$115, 036, 361 (Worldwide)
Tagline	A story about how far we must travel to find the place where we belong.

"Superb performances by Tobey Maguire and Michael Caine bring a bracing sense of humanity to the story…" David Sterritt, *Christian Science Monitor*

"Guided by Mr. Hallström and anchored by Mr. Irving, *The Cider House Rules* achieves a lovely unity that's rare in such an episodic movie." Philip Wuntch, *Dallas Morning News*

This was the start of the end. Suddenly the director of the fantastic *What's Eating Gilbert Grape* (1993) and the sublime *My Life as a Dog* (1996) (not to mention the master behind *Abba: The Movie* (1977)) becomes a slushy American. I suppose it gets to everyone eventually – even Hitchcock had to come back to England at the end of his career to make some more decent movies. But it comes as a real shame for Hallström, who had so much promise … but after this pile of overrated nonsense he went on to kill *The Shipping News* (2001) and make *Casanova* (2005) bland.

So how did *The Cider House Rules* manage to get festooned with awards and plaudits? The film is twee and sugary sweet, with no backbone or even a proper story to follow. Perhaps the powers that be hoped that if they supported Lasse then he would come back to form again? Or maybe it was some evil CIA plot to "Americanize" the director, and stop him making films that were original, thought-provoking and faintly subversive.

Whatever it was, the scheme worked. Michael Caine's pathetic attempt at an American accent alone should have condemned *The Cider House Rules* to the straight to video shelf. Tobey Maguire nearly killed off a promising career by playing the young amateur abortionist who wants to be an apple farmer (honestly!) – thankfully a starring role in *Ride with the Devil* (1999) at the same time saved him.

Be warned, this is totally sentimental tosh that does not deserve a viewing. Lasse, you made a real dog.

Clerks

A day in the life of two convenience store clerks as they discuss love, sport and other issues (and try to keep their friends in check).

Director	Kevin Smith
Writer	Kevin Smith
Starring	Brian O'Halloran
	Jeff Anderson
Released	1994
Awards	Two awards at Cannes, one at Deauville, one at Sundance. Six assorted nominations.
Box office	Worldwide US$ figure unavailable
Tagline	Just because they serve you … doesn't mean they like you.

"Screw the bad acting. Forget the poor production values. Never mind that the plot is barely existent. *Clerks* is funny. We're talking spit-out-your-food, snort-out-your-milk funny. We're talking exchange-lines-with-your-friends-years-after-you've-seen-it funny. And to think: it only cost about $23,000 to make." Elbert Ventura, *Campus Nut*

There are some things I just don't get. I don't think Angelina Jolie is attractive (she's an anorexic hamster on stilts), I cannot be bothered looking at My Space (get some real friends you losers), and I really, really cannot fathom why Kevin Smith is allowed to make movies. This is a man I would not put in charge of the remote control of my VCR. He has little style, no humour, and an amazing dearth where cinematic talent should be.

But suddenly he makes a low-budget film that is so desperate not to appear to be trying too hard that it almost has a hernia, and he's the bright new thing. Internet geeks love Kevin Smith – they see someone who's cool and seemingly has friends and a life (unlike themselves). The reputation took off and the rest is (shameful) history ... *Mallrats* (1995), *Chasing Amy* (1997), the quite horrific *Dogma* (1999) and, of course, Ben Affleck's finest moment, *Jersey Girl* (2004). OK *Gigli* (2003) might have been worse, but most of us didn't have to suffer that.

So let me say again – I do not get Kevin Smith. And I certainly do not get *Clerks*. It's just not funny. The style is self-consciously shambolic. The jokes aren't funny. The in-jokes aren't funny. The characters aren't funny. I can honestly say that I sat through the whole 92 minutes (it seemed much longer) without even cracking a smile.

But, thanks to our friends who are married to their computers we've not only had *Clerks*, we've had *Jay and Silent Bob Strike Back* (2001) – another laugh-a-century movie – and, God help us, *Clerks II* (2006).

So if you've got a life, and some friends, please remember that this film is not for you. But if you're going to live with your mother until she dies, and possibly for a couple of weeks after that, then this is your movie Nirvana.

Close My Eyes

A brother and sister break one of the oldest taboos and embark on a sexual relationship.

Director	Stephen Poliakoff
Writer	Stephen Poliakoff
Starring	Alan Rickman
	Clive Owen
	Saskia Reeves
Released	1991
Awards	Best Film, and Best Actor for Alan Rickman at the Evening Standard Awards. Alan Rickman also won British Actor of the Year at the London Critics Circle Film Awards, and Best Actor at the Seattle International Film Festival.
Box office	Worldwide US$ figure unavailable

"Poliakoff's challenging human drama dares to confront highly sensitive issues including Aids and the taboo subject of incest, and uses the themes as melancholic metaphors for the irresponsible self-indulgence of the Thatcherite 1980s." (uncredited) Britmovie.co.uk

Oh didn't the chattering classes of London's Islington love this film? They cooed about Poliakoff's analogy about the yuppie culture (and Aids, and everything else afflicting modern man), they gasped at the sexual intensity and they boasted how they were able to face up to the taboo that is incest.

I have to admit I only went to see it for one reason – Saskia Reeves naked. In fact why they didn't put this on the poster I don't know (movie marketers eh? Haven't a clue). And she did get naked … very naked. After admiring the actress from afar (*December Bride* (1990)) quite frankly, as they say, I wanted to see more. But what sort of director is Poliakoff (obviously not his real name)? The more naked good old Saskia got, the more unattractive she appeared. In fact, and I hate to say it, she looked like a normal person. That's not what I pay my admission price for sir.

But even if you didn't just go to see Saskia Curves (sorry Reeves), and I'm told that some didn't (maybe they wanted to see Clive Owen naked instead?), you have to admit that this is a load of old tosh. The director has a habit of trying to fool the audience into thinking that he's profound by using long lingering shots of architecture for no apparent reason. For future reference: this is because he didn't shoot enough action or story to last the 90 minutes – he might as well have had the pussycat playing with the ball of string.

The dialogue, as with all of Poliakoff's work, is pompous and laughable. Again, he is so po-faced that he manages to fool some people. But the language, when looked at in depth, has no real substance or function. And God is it annoying.

At least he got the title right: close my eyes? I wanted to close my ears too. And never forget this is the man who also gave us Anna Friel naked in *The Tribe* (1999) … so he does horror too.

Closer

The lives of two couples intertwine – Daniel loves Alice, but then makes a pass at Anna, who he later sets up with Larry. Dan and Anna then start an affair that pushes Alice and Larry together too.

Director	Mike Nichols
Writer	Patrick Marber (from his play)
Starring	Natalie Portman
	Jude Law
	Julia Roberts
	Clive Owen
Released	2004
Awards	A BAFTA, two Golden Globes, and five film critic society awards. 19 nominations including for two Oscars.
Box office	$101,487,757 (Worldwide)
Tagline	If you believe in love at first sight, you never stop looking.

"The film is an emotional Rorschach test for viewers, suggesting a sadly diminishing role for affection and trust in modern relationships." Jack Garner, *Rochester Democrat and Chronicle*

"Closer is a startling and fascinating film that is both revealing and challenging, as it toys with the enormity of love and commitment." Louise Keller, Urban Cinefile (Australia)

Many talk about Orson Welles starting at the top with *Citizen Kane* (1941) and then going downhill. How do you think Mike Nichols feels? This is the man who began life in pre-war Germany with the name Michael Igor Peschkowsky, but still managed to launch his directing career with *Who's Afraid of Virginia Woolf?* (1966), *The Graduate* (1967), *Catch-22* (1970) and *Carnal Knowledge* (1971). And now he's pushing this load of pretentious nonsense. He'd be better off doing sherry commercials.

Closer is a bad play that makes for even worse cinema. Navel-gazing at its highest (or should I say lowest?), the film was praised for saying so much about relationships. But the truth is, if it says anything to you about a relationship it actually means that you've never been in one. Dialogue-heavy and horribly stylized, *Closer* is not set in the real world. Let's be honest, the stripper doesn't even take her clothes off.

This was an excuse for four famous actors to demonstrate that they're not just pretty faces. And all they ended up proving was that they're not even pretty faces. The acting is wooden, even taking into consideration that they had little to work with (please note scriptwriter Patrick Marber, big words don't always equate with intelligence).

Closer is not funny, it's not sexy (or sensual) and it definitely isn't honest. The film is little more than middle-class wish fulfilment (oh don't we all wish we had to choose between Natalie Portman and Julia Roberts). It really is Mamet-lite.

The Constant Gardener

A mild-mannered diplomat in Nairobi tries to discover the details behind his wife's death, and in the process opens a political can of worms.

Director	Fernando Meirelles
Writer	Jeffrey Caine (from John le Carré's book)
Starring	Ralph Fiennes
	Rachel Weisz
	Hubert Koundé
Released	2005
Awards	Rachel Weisz won an Oscar, and the film got three nominations. One BAFTA, and 9 nominations. Three British Independent Film Awards and four nominations. The list goes on…
Box office	Worldwide US$ figure unavailable
Tagline	Love. At any cost.

"It is not just an intricate, despairing meditation on the shabby compromises involved in maintaining Britain's interests and waning foreign prestige. There is real anger here, and a real sense that it is worthwhile striking back against wrongdoing."
Peter Bradshaw, *Guardian*

Guess what? There's a lot of rather nasty big business type people in Africa, who are exploiting the locals. And worse, the politicians know about it!

There, that's saved you over two hours of tedium (you'll never have that time again you know). Because *The Constant Gardener* has little else to say – there are not even any horticultural tips. From the director who gave us *City of God* (2002), and a story adapted from the novel by John le Carré, this is a major disappointment. But a disappointment it is, let's move on and not try to dress up a pig as "The Rose of Tralee".

At very best *The Constant Gardener* is average, although I do think that Ralph Fiennes attempting "emotional" drags it way down below that. The spirited Rachel Weisz soldiers on gamely to do what she can with poor and obvious material. But the film is inconsequential and unimpressive. Perhaps its champions feel that it may be racist to criticize a movie about Africa and Aids, directed by a Brazilian. Or maybe they just dropped off in the middle, and so thought it easier to acclaim it.

Whatever it was (and I'm sure that le Carré could get a good conspiracy theory out of it), the plaudits *The Constant Gardener* received are completely baffling. *Shooting Dogs* (2005), *Hotel Rwanda* (2004) and *Tsotsi* (2005) have all shown the potential of African cinema. But *The Constant Gardener* is simply too much manure and certainly doesn't come up smelling of roses.

The Cook, the Thief, His Wife & Her Lover

The trophy wife of a brutish gangster and restaurant-owner goes looking for love elsewhere, with horrific consequences.

Director	Peter Greenaway
Writer	Peter Greenaway
Starring	Richard Bohringer
	Michael Gambon
	Helen Mirren
Released	1989
Awards	Won all its categories (four) at the Catalonian International Film Festival, Best Foreign Film at the Chicago Film Critics Association awards, and got three other nominations.
Box office	Worldwide US$ figure unavailable
Tagline	Lust … Murder … Dessert. Bon appetit!

"British director Peter Greenaway is audacious enough to stage a metaphor so grand, so lavishly comprehensive, that it can stand as a final, definitive assessment of the state of Western civilization." Hal Hinson, *Washington Post*

101 Movies to Avoid could almost be made up entirely of Peter Greenaway movies. Thankfully now even the most pretentious of movie snobs have realized that they're backing a loser, but rare was the voice against this "auteur" in the 1990s (have you notice how similar "artistic" and "autistic" are? Surely no coincidence?). Alan Parker said that he would pack up and leave the country if Peter Greenaway ever made another film. Sadly he didn't keep his promise (holding out for his knighthood perhaps), and has not made a good film himself since, but fair play to him for speaking out against this old nonsense when everyone else was scared of looking silly.

If you weren't around in the 1980s and 90s (or at least not old enough to go to any film without checking the certificate) it's hard to imagine just what snobbery there was about Greenaway, which came to a pinnacle during the release of The Cook, the Thief, His Wife & Her Lover (no game of charades was complete without someone trying to mime this title). Nobody had the nerve to ask "what is this load of old tosh about?" for fear of looking stupid (never mind that everyone was wearing pastel suits and shirts buttoned to the top with no tie).

Thankfully the great movie public actually led the way. Despite the reverence paid to Greenaway from all corners of Islington, no one actually went to see his movies. This of course is a double-edged sword, as our taxes then had to go to finance his work ("you don't need another hospital, you would much rather have an allegory on the human psyche played out in different colours for each emotion"). But eventually the extremely dense film community got the message and thankfully his work has hardly seen a cinema this century.

I'll actually say very little about The Cook ... except to mention how scandalous it is to have Michael Gambon, Helen Mirren and Tim Roth together and make such a heap of nonsense.

The Crying Game

An IRA terrorist befriends a soldier that he has kidnapped, and gets drawn into a strange world of love and deceit.

Director	Neil Jordan
Writer	Neil Jordan
Starring	Forest Whitaker
	Miranda Richardson
	Stephen Rea
	Jaye Davidson
Released	1992
Awards	Oscar for Best Screenplay, and five nominations. One BAFTA for Best British Film, and six nominations. Another 16 wins, and five more nominations.
Box office	Worldwide US$ figure unavailable
Tagline	The movie everyone is talking about… But no one is giving away its secrets.

"A corker from start to finish with its exploration of the choices which define the soul." Frederic and Mary Ann Brussat, *Spirituality and Practice*

"… one of the most challenging, surprising films of the year…" Hal Hinson, *Washington Post*

The girl's got a dick.

There we go, I've just saved you two hours of your life. For there is little else notable about *The Crying Game* except for this cynical and simplistic device. And it's not even that good a twist. In a bar, after six or seven pints, you might (just might) think that Jaye Davidson looks a bit of all right. But stone cold sober, watching him on a huge cinema screen, you're never going to be fooled. Are you?

The Crying Game was loaded with awards and critical acclaim which must really piss off genuinely creative film makers that try to make interesting and challenging movies rather than just casting a bloke who looks vaguely feminine (to me Boy George was much harder to guess).

The only other thing worth talking about in the movie (see one Neil Jordan you've seen 'em all – lots of poignant silent moments, crass attempts at analysing the world, Stephen Rea looking like a bulldog with a wasp in his mouth) is Miranda Richardson's woeful Irish accent. Many have challenged for worst Irish accent on screen, and dishonourable mentions must go to Sadie Frost in *Shopping* (1994) and Emily Lloyd in *When Saturday Comes* (1996), but the award can only belong to Richardson. A talented comedy actress, my only conclusion is that she misread (or maybe not) the script and thought it a pastiche.

But at least she's not got a dick.

Dead Poets Society

An unconventional teacher inspires his class to embrace poetry and to "seize the day", much to the chagrin of his stuffy employers.

Director	Peter Weir
Writer	Tom Schulman
Starring	Robin Williams
	Robert Sean Leonard
	Ethan Hawke
Released	1989
Awards	An Oscar for the screenplay, and three nominations. Two BAFTAs including Best Film and four nominations. A César for Best Foreign Film, the Gold Film Award from the Guild of German Art House Cinemas, and so on…
Box office	$235,900,000 (Worldwide)
Tagline	He was their inspiration. He made their lives extraordinary.

"As consistent and nearly as understated a performance as Robin Williams would give later in *Good Will Hunting*." James Plath, Reel.com

Warning – Robin Williams in "earnest" mode. And there's few things worse, cinematically speaking, than Robin Williams being intense (except, of course, when he's trying to be funny).

Dead Poets Society really is a poor film (they didn't even bother putting an apostrophe into the title, which shows the lack of care and attention in the script!). Inspiring? Surely some mistake. Williams is nauseating, irritating, exasperating … he's a lot of things, but inspiring he's not. To a country as stupid as America (what's the difference between the US and a yogurt? A yogurt's got culture) it might seem as if the teacher is expanding his young students' (can the makers of this film please note the use of the apostrophe) minds. In the UK he would probably be put onto a register.

The pompous attitude throughout this dirge really makes *Dead Poets Society* unbearable. This is the sort of nonsense that could only appeal to the geeky kid at school who keeps his dinner money in a purse and has a string connecting his gloves. Poetry is not fun, or inspiring; in fact most of it is quite boring (and a lot of the modern stuff doesn't even rhyme).

Williams himself is so sanctimonious and self-righteous that you're glad when he finally gets the push. I have no idea why the kids stood on the tables at the end – it's the sort of thing you do when you're 12 and then cringe about for the rest of your life.

Dead Poets Society definitely inspired me … mostly to shout at the screen and vow to poke earnest Robin Williams in the eye should I ever meet him. It is interesting that he previously appeared in a film called *Seize the Day* (1986) … seize him by the neck more like it.

La Dolce Vita

A playboy journalist wafts his way around the Roman social scene.

Director	Federico Fellini
Writers	Federico Fellini, Ennio Flaiano, Tullio Pinelli, Brunello Rondi
Starring	Marcello Mastroianni
	Anita Ekberg
	Anouk Aimee
Released	1960
Awards	Oscar for Best Costume Design, and three nominations, won the Golden Palm at Cannes and three Silver Ribbons from the Italian National Syndicate of Film Journalists.
Box office	Worldwide US$ figure unavailable
Tagline	The Roman Scandals – Bound to shock with its truth!

"[Fellini's] poetic sensibilities are in full effect. There's also a tremendous soulfulness that roots the movie's depiction of sin in the soil of introspection." Wesley Morris, *Boston Globe*

"*La Dolce Vita* is still a potent, expressionistic launch into post-war Euro-emptiness…" Michael Atkinson, *Village Voice*

You could guess that anyone calling themselves Federico would be pretentious. What's wrong with good old Fred as a name, eh? And that surname? Obviously made up (probably got something to do with an unnatural liking for cats).

Some people can't decide whether this is neo-realist or fantasy. Can't they spell "shit"? Nice opening shot of Christ leaving Rome (although done much better in *LA Story* (1991)), and then nearly three hours of bum-numbing inconsequential fluff. Yes, I know the film is supposed to be about a vacuous life, but I really don't want to spend my time watching trivial and insignificant events.

The trouble is that people have been told for so long that this is a masterpiece they now believe it. It's easier, isn't it? Most people that recommend *La Dolce Vita* to you will probably never have seen it – or maybe they went along, and then filled in the three hours by having a wee nap.

Well it's time to stand up and proclaim against this trivial nonsense masquerading as "art". Say it loud, say it proud, *La Dolce Vita* is tedious. Just because it's in black and white, and a foreign language, doesn't make it any better.

The Italians are very good at certain things (ice cream, clothes, football, wars … OK, maybe not wars). But far too much importance and praise has been heaped upon Italian post-war cinema. Some of it isn't bad (Fellini's *I Viteloni* (1953) and Visconti's *Rocco e I suoi Fratelli* (1960) among them). But a lot is overindulgent dross. And *La Dolce Vita* definitely falls into this category.

Dr. Strangelove: or How I Stopped Worrying and Learned to Love the Bomb

A nuclear war seems imminent as a rogue general goes off the rails; a room full of politicians and military top brass convene to try to avoid Armageddon.

Director	Stanley Kubrick
Writer	Stanley Kubrick
Starring	Peter Sellers
	George C. Scott
	Sterling Hayden
Released	1964
Awards	Won four BAFTAs, including two Best Film awards, and three nominations. Nominated for four Oscars.
Box office	Worldwide US$ figure unavailable
Tagline	The hot-line suspense comedy.

"It's one of the greatest – and undoubtedly the most hilarious – antiwar statements ever put to film. See it before the world ends." Marjorie Baumgarten, *Austin Chronicle*

"One of Kubrick's greatest films." Brian McKay, EFilmcritic.com, Rotten Tomatoes

Everyone needs somebody beside them to say "no" occasionally. In my case it's my wife ("no you won't have the extra drink", "no you can't stay in bed any longer, there's a mortgage to be paid" etc.), for others it might be a business partner, a boss or just a best friend. Sadly Kubrick had no one to say "no" to him on the set of *Dr. Strangelove* (we'll ignore the rest of the title, which someone should definitely have said "no" to).

What could have been a clever broad satire that's not afraid to take risks thus disappeared right up the director's rear. People think they must like *Dr. Strangelove* or they'll be thought of as dour or unintelligent. Relax, you're allowed to hate it – I won't think any less of you. Promise.

Peter Sellers hams it up terribly (I suppose if no one was saying "no" to Kubrick, he didn't want to impose rules on anyone else), yet got tremendous acclaim just because he wore some different hats.

What should have been a short *Spitting Image* sketch is stretched out to fill an hour and a half. It's all overblown, overacted, and not terribly funny.

Yes Kubrick was a great director. But this is nowhere near his finest moment. He needed a strong producer to rein him in, but the producer was … Stanley Kubrick. He could do horror (*The Shining* (1980) is still guaranteed to send a shiver down your spine), he could do war (*Full Metal Jacket* (1987) being one of the best ever), he could do nearly everything. But comedy? No, no, no, no, no. The man just didn't have a sense of humour … but then again, he did direct *Eyes Wide Shut* (1999).

Dirty Dancing

A teenage girl goes to a holiday camp in the 1950s and comes out a woman, thanks to her encounter with a sexy dance instructor.

Director	Emile Ardolino
Writer	Eleanor Bergstein
Starring	Jennifer Grey
	Patrick Swayze
	Jerry Orbach
Released	1987
Awards	Oscar and Golden Globe for Best Original Song. Nominated for the Critics award at Deauville Film Festival.
Box office	$170,292,689 (Worldwide)
Tagline	First dance. First love. The time of your life.

"There are only a few basic irrefutable truths in the known universe. One of them just happens to be that nobody puts Baby in the corner." Clare, *Mutant Reviewers From Hell*

Overrated? *Dirty Dancing*? "No" I hear you all cry. And I grant that it was not a critical success on release. But to the army of devoted fans (mostly women, with a few "men in uncomfortable shoes") it's not just a film, it's a religion. They quote the lines ad nauseam and wax lyrical about how the picture changed their lives. It's their fault that we had a sequel and a stage show. It's also their fault that you're humming "oh, the time of my life, no I've never felt like this before" just now.

But these people don't deserve punishment, they need help. They really need someone to point out them that *Dirty Dancing* is a fairly predictable, cheesy and unoriginal flick that should have had no more than a couple of weeks in the cinema and then be banished to the furthest shelf in the DVD rental store.

Swayze is terrible, naturally (he has one facial expression that he uses for every emotion, which looks like he's suffering from wind and trying to sneak one out). Jennifer Grey was in reality no "Baby," she was actually 27 when she shot the film, and the dialogue is truly atrocious (cringeworthy the whole way through).

So what is the attraction to this rather than the superior teen flicks of the time (like the wonderful *Footloose* (1984) and little Tom's big break in *Risky Business* (1983))? It must be a girl thing, because I just can't see it at all (maybe they put odour of chocolate through the air conditioning of the cinemas, or perhaps there's some subliminal message in the film about shoes or shopping).

To me it still remains a shoddy film (it looks like the cameraman put orange cellophane over the lens). Put Baby in a corner? I would prefer to put her in a cupboard and lock the door.

Election

Tracy Flick will do anything to win the school election, and her teacher will try everything to ensure she doesn't.

Director	Alexander Payne
Writers	Alexander Payne, Jim Taylor, (from Tom Perrotta's book)
Starring	Matthew Broderick
	Reese Witherspoon
	Chris Klein
Released	1999
Awards	15 awards including three Independent Spirit Awards for Best Feature, Director and Screenplay, eight Critics' awards, a Writers Guild of America award, and Best Casting from the Casting Society of America.14 nominations including an Oscar nomination for the Screenplay and a Golden Globe for Best Actress.
Box office	$15,979,556 (Worldwide)
Tagline	Reading, writing, revenge.

"... a teen comedy with a sophisticated adult edge. Like *Heathers* or *Fast Times at Ridgemont High*, it transcends the genre." Jack Garner, *Rochester Democrat and Chronicle*

For a short while you were a social outcast if you hadn't seen *Election*, and proclaimed it the most inventive and blackest comedy ever, ever, ever made. Hopefully like Rubik's cubes and ra-ra skirts people will now look back and wonder why.

Election is a fairly run-of-the mill attempt at comedy. It's not that it's terrible – it's just average, and no more. Someone actually had the cheek to suggest recently that it is an underrated movie. I don't think so!

So please, answers on a postcard, where is this great underlying intelligence that everyone goes on about? Where's the wicked satire and subversive message? You can't tell me because they're not really there. It's just that so many people told you that they were they you were afraid to say otherwise.

Put *Election* against seriously intelligent high school comedies (particularly *10 Things I Hate About You* (1999), which also had a much better soundtrack) and it shrinks by comparison.

Reese Witherspoon showed what a great actress she is in *Walk the Line* (2005) and *Sweet Home Alabama* (2002). But in *Election* she is still young, and given such an outrageous role she simply chews the scenery. Matthew Broderick similarly shows why he's someone's husband now (don't even think of getting me started about *The Producers* (2005)).

Putting the record straight once and for all then: *Election* has two or three laughs, and passes the time well enough. But it is no work of genius by any stretch of the imagination. I do wish people would stop looking for hidden depths when no such depths exist.

The English Patient

As the war nears its end a nurse cares for a badly burnt man; slowly his past is revealed and we see the loves and betrayal that have hurt him more than the airplane crash he suffered.

Director	Anthony Minghella
Writer	Anthony Minghella, (from Michael Ondaatje's book)
Starring	Ralph Fiennes
	Juliette Binoche
	Willem Dafoe
	Kristin Scott Thomas
Released	1996
Awards	Won nine Oscars including Best Picture and Director, and nominated for three further awards. Won six BAFTAs including Best Film, and nominated for seven more. In fact it won or was nominated for just about everything going.
Box office	$231,700,000
Tagline	In memory, love lives forever.

"Winner of nine Oscars in all, the film should be seen several times. On each viewing, more detail is obvious, more emotion palpable, and a genuine feeling towards the characters comes through." Ali Barclay, BBCi

Slow, slow, slow, slow, slow. In fact, to call *The English Patient* slow is like saying that Gene Kelly liked a wee dance. This movie takes slow to another static level never before quarried by films. It is slower than a train on a Sunday afternoon, slower than a slug taking his time, slower than Nicolas Cage reciting a very long poem.

Like a slide show of a neighbour's vacation, the audience are supposed to feign interest as yet another long lingering shot shows Fiennes in the desert. But it's from a book, so it must be good – right? Big wrong I'm afraid. Watching *The English Patient* is like falling down the stairs. It is an experience, not one that you're likely to forget, but similarly not one you ever want to repeat.

We were bombarded at the time with ridiculous praise for this bore-a-thon. "Isn't the photography beautiful?" Once you've seen one desert you've seen 'em all really. "It is so clever the way they tell the story in flashback." Not really – it's hardly original and the device is not handled well by Minghella. "Aren't the performances magnificent?" Most of the acting is uninspiring, and the less said about Kristin Scott Thomas in the bath the better (Minghella is obsessed with women in the bath; in *Breaking and Entering* (2006) he places Juliette Binoche and Robin Wright Penn in baths at different times).

If you escaped the hype and managed to miss *The English Patient* the first time around, well done. To the rest of you … well, think of it as the closest you will get to a comatose state without having to go to hospital.

And did I mention that it was slow?

Fahrenheit 9/11

The controversial director's take on 9/11 and the Bush Presidency.

Director	Michael Moore
Writer	Michael Moore
Starring	Ben Affleck
	Stevie Wonder
	George W. Bush
Released	2004
Awards	Won, among others, the Golden Palm at Cannes and several Critics' Associations awards, but also four Razzies for the "acting" of, for example, George W. Bush.
Box office	$220,078,393
Tagline	The temperature where freedom burns!

"If 2004 is the year of the documentary, Michael Moore's Palme d'Or-winning *Fahrenheit 9/11* is undoubtedly doc of the year... It's also the film the powers-that-be didn't want you to see – an incendiary, raging epic that will do more to scupper George Bush's re-election hopes than anything the Democrats could dream up." Jamie Russell, BBCi

Congratulations Mr. Moore, you got George W. Bush elected for a second term. For once in America's history the population were willing to listen to someone slightly left of centre, and you blew it. *Fahrenheit 9/11* could have done so much for the world (and saved so many lives). For a change cinema was actually important. But instead of making a reasoned documentary telling the people of the good old U S of A truths that they won't hear on Fox News, Moore decided to turn the film into one long polemical rant.

Instead of focusing on one issue, and God knows there is enough to work on with Bush in the White House, the chubby TV presenter (for that's all he really is – check out *Canadian Bacon* (1995) if you're ever tempted to think of him as an actual film maker) just delivered a scattergun diatribe. There was no focus or direction to the film, and no real point to be made except that Michael Moore knows everything and George W. is a bad man. No big revelations that we didn't know, no real search for the truth or even interesting and coherent arguments.

The media intelligentsia of course loved it. Why? Because he was singing to the choir. But I can't imagine that one person who was going to vote Bush changed their mind after seeing this. For a start it's not even a documentary. Moore's work in general is so contrived and set up that it's embarrassing he should think he's fooling anyone. If there's something he doesn't agree with, it doesn't get into the final cut. In his previous movie *Bowling for Columbine* (2002), Moore proclaimed that nobody in Canada locked their front doors and showed a montage of him gaining entry to surprised Canucks' homes. When pushed about this segment he proudly proclaimed that six out of ten doors he tried were unlocked. Then show the other four Michael, and you might just change something instead of simply blowing up your ego.

Four Weddings and a Funeral

Charles is besotted with a beautiful and mysterious American woman who he meets at the constant stream of social events his friends invite him to.

Director	Mike Newell
Writer	Richard Curtis
Starring	Hugh Grant
	James Fleet
	Simon Callow
Released	1994
Awards	Four BAFTAs including Best Film and Best Actor, and nominated for seven more. Won a British Comedy Award, a César, three Evening Standard awards and a Golden Globe. Nominated for a number of awards including two Oscars.
Box office	$244,100,000
Tagline	He's quite engaging. She's otherwise engaged.

"As for the central affair … it's made doubly charming by Grant and MacDowell (whose extraordinary face and presence more than justify his romantic obsession). They so obviously belong to each other … you're kept at the edge of your pew until the very last moment." Desson Howe, *Washington Post*

I love romantic comedies. I in particular love Working Title romantic comedies. Over the years I have even got to love Hugh Grant. But cannot for the life of me see how *Four Weddings and a Funeral* managed to kick the whole phenomena into life.

It's a horrible, sloppy and quite unfunny film. The one decent joke was used to death on the various TV shows in advance so failed to raise a giggle when we finally got to see it. The movie has no class, no charm and very little story to talk of.

If it wasn't for those damned Americans. The film opened in the US first (a very brave move at the time) and probably would have sunk without a trace (although Liz Hurley's breasts contributed to keeping it afloat too). But, cynically, this is the England that America wants to see (not intelligent dramas set in council estates). And as the Yanks don't really have a sense of humour (have you ever noticed that they will nod and say something like "that's funny" instead of laughing?) so this was perfect for them.

By the time *Four Weddings…* arrived in the UK you simply had to see it; and you had to enjoy it. Try to watch it again, away from the hysteria, and you will wonder what you ever saw in it. Andie MacDowell is a lifeless lump of wood and Hugh Grant is toadying (a bit like Uriah Heep on acid).

But look at the bright side, if you hadn't been hoodwinked by *Four Weddings…* then we would never have been treated to Kirsten Dunst in a tennis skirt in *Wimbledon* (2004). At least Kristin Scott Thomas doesn't have a bath, and Liz Hurley isn't in it (strange how she can help a film so much by not appearing in it – but then if you've seen *Passenger 57* (1992) you'll understand why).

Gangs of New York

As the Irish gangs fight to establish a power basis in their new city a young man seeks revenge for his father's death.

Director	Martin Scorsese
Writers	Jay Cocks, Steven Zaillian, Kenneth Lonergan,
Starring	Leonardo DiCaprio
	Daniel Day Lewis
	Cameron Diaz
Released	2002
Awards	33 awards and 65 nominations, including 10 Oscar nominations. Martin Scorsese won a Golden Globe, as did U2 for Best Original Song. Daniel Day-Lewis won a BAFTA, an award from the Screen Actors Guild, as well as plenty from Film Critics Circles.
Box office	US$190, 379,638
Tagline	America was born in the streets.

"Indeed, it's something of the ultimate Scorsese film, with all the stomach-turning violence, colorful New York gang lore and other hallmarks of his personal cinema painted on their largest-ever historical canvas." William Arnold, *Seattle Post-Intelligencer*

My oh my. What can you say about *Gangs of New York* that doesn't have the words "laughable" and "preposterous" in it? Much was made of the time of Scorsese's insistence that he doesn't use CGI and all the locations and thousands of extras were actually present and real. If only he had spent as much time on script and direction and we could have had a decent movie.

Instead we have a cast of thousands in what can only described as a dog. It's Marty, so people will always love it and throw awards at it. But that goodwill is going to stop any day now Mr. Scorsese. And once you're assessed on a level playing ground people will start to see what utter garbage *Gangs of New York* is.

You can't really help Leonardo DiCaprio (although you didn't have to cast him Marty) – he's weak; always has been and always will be. There's more depth in a kiddies' paddling pool than in his performance and his girlie good looks are so out of kilter with his supposed character. But what the hell was Daniel Day Lewis doing (or at least trying to do) with Bill the Butcher? Ironically he truly butchered the role with a ham-fisted, over the top portrayal that gets on your nerves from the first second. He is a moustache-twirling villain of the old hackneyed school. Apparently the method actor spent months learning to be a butcher, if only he had spent some time training to be an actor.

Poor old Liam Neeson and Cameron Diaz struggle on manfully, but there is little you can do when you've got one lead that's less visible than Casper the friendly ghost, and the other one mugging you for every scene.

Scorsese does make it look like an epic, and thus managed to fool some people into thinking that there was some merit and depth here. But it's a smoke-and-mirrors trick. The film isn't that violent, says nothing about modern America, and even the dirt looks false.

Please – give it up Mr. Scorsese while people still like you!

Ghost

A murdered man must come back to warn his fiancée of the imminent danger she faces.

Director	Jerry Zucker
Writer	Bruce Joel Rubin
Starring	Patrick Swayze
	Demi Moore
	Tony Goldwyn
Released	1990
Awards	Two Oscars (Best Screenplay and Best Supporting Actress for Whoopi Goldberg), and nominated for three further awards. Whoopi Goldberg also won a Golden Globe, a BAFTA, an American Comedy Award, and several others. 16 wins and 20 nominations in total.
Box office	$517,600,000
Tagline	Before Sam was murdered he told Molly he'd love and protect her. Forever.

"A wonderful movie, sincere and inspired, with four terrific performances and a story that doesn't let up. The picture has the gentle, nourishing quality of a fairy tale that you want to believe, and the unsoftened impact of gut-level entertainment."
Mick LaSalle, *San Francisco Chronicle*

Oh my God this is a truly dreadful film in every way, and a huge disappointment considering it's from the man who helped give us *Airplane* (1980).

Demi – stop crying and do something with that hair. Patrick, put some Polyfilla on the face and try some acting lessons. Whoopi … oh, what's the point? The poor girl's career is over now anyway. But you did make me suffer and I won't forget it.

Essentially a 1980s movie (from the bad hair-dos to the corporate big business shenanigans), the film was already out of date when it was released in 1990. But people flocked to it. The Academy even gave it an Oscar for, wait for it, Best Screenplay! This is particularly perplexing as the only piece people remember is Demi spinning her potter's wheel (as you do in your front room) while *Unchained Melody* plays relentlessly in the background.

There is a phoniness that pervades *Ghost*. It is not touching and romantic as many (mostly women – something to do with their hormones probably) state. The relationship between the two leads is cold and unengaging. This is not a story that stands up to scrutiny (Why is he still around? Why aren't there other ghosts? What is all that rubbish about him learning to touch things? How is Whoopi Goldberg helping?). Suspension of disbelief, essential to all good movies, is impossible here with just too many questions going through your mind.

Ghost is a sloppy and cynical tearjerker that should be ashamed of itself (playing on the emotions of dumped, or just fat and ugly, women). If you want a good sloppy movie watch *Beaches* (1988) – better acting, better story, and a much better song (and not a potter's wheel in sight).

Girl with a Pearl Earring

A fictional tale of what might have been the story behind Vermeer's famous painting.

Director	Peter Webber
Writer	Olivia Hetreed (from Tracy Chevalier's book)
Starring	Colin Firth
	Scarlett Johansson
	Tom Wilkinson
Released	2003
Awards	Won 11 awards, mostly for the cinematography.
	Nominated for three Oscars and 10 BAFTAs.
Box office	Worldwide US$ figure unavailable
Tagline	Beauty inspires obsession.

"*Girl with a Pearl Earring* is a stolen glimpse around dark doorways into the intense, colorful birth of a great creation."
Anita Schmaltz, *Metro Times Detroit*

The perfect film for the pseudo intellectual – the kind of people who like to pretend they know what they're talking about and have good taste. So they cannot but run to a movie such as *Girl with a Pearl Earring* – it's about art after all.

Honestly, stop yourself now and just think for a minute. Vermeer is hardly a genius. His work is only one step up from the boy with the candle and the tennis player scratching her bum. It's the kind of "art" that people get when they buy their own council house and think they've moved up the social order (a Vermeer print and an oak front door come automatically with the lease I believe).

So not only are we dealing with a fairly ordinary painter, but this is not even the true story of his life and art. It's all made up – a work of fiction that comes from a fairly ordinary book (again, only one step up from Jackie Collins but the novel has real pretensions).

However, if the film had been any good I would have forgiven all this. But it's ponderous nonsense. With her hair pulled back and hidden in the period costume Scarlett looks sadly like Daffy Duck's paler sister. Colin Firth strides around the set like a man who knows his one role was on telly more than 10 years before. The chemistry between them is simply not there.

There's a lot of standing in dark corners watching wistfully, and panning shots that basically just point out that the production only had a couple of sets (you want to shoot a movie about Amsterdam, so you go to Luxemburg – where else?). The lighting and production design aren't bad, and Tom Wilkinson makes a spirited bid to try to make the film interesting, but that isn't really enough.

As fake as the story it is based on, this is truly a film for those who don't understand what they're watching, but desperately want the world to think of them as connoisseurs.

Gods and Monsters

A friendship develops between the very camp director of *Frankenstein* and his ex-Marine gardener.

Director	Bill Condon
Writer	Bill Condon (from Christopher Bram's book *Father of Frankenstein*)
Starring	Ian McKellen
	Brendan Fraser
	Lynn Redgrave
	Lolita Davidovich
Released	1998
Awards	An Oscar for Best Screenplay, and Ian McKellen and Lynn Redgrave were nominated. Lynn Redgrave won a Golden Globe, and she and Ian McKellen and the film won Independent Spirit awards. In total, 33 wins and 23 nominations.
Box office	Worldwide US$ figure unavailable

"Bill Condon's *Gods and Monsters* is a nearly perfect movie. When film historians write the cinematic history of this decade, it will surely be included." Bob Stephens, *San Francisco Examiner*

There are some people that really should come out of the closet. Come on guys, it's the 21st century. You're not fooling anyone with the slinky babes on your arm at the premieres. We can take it. However Sir Ian McKellen should be shoved back into the aforementioned closet. Ian, we get the point. We know you're gay. We don't care, but you're really starting to bore us. It's time you were "inned".

And *Gods and Monsters* really is a load of camp old nonsense. What a waste of the brilliant Brendan Fraser's time – he could have been doing another *George of the Jungle* (1997) instead (which the world would have thanked him for). Desperately trying to steal some of the old Hollywood essence that exudes from fare such as *Sunset Boulevard* (1950), *Gods and Monsters* simply tries too hard. The film doth protest too much – it is literally screaming that this isn't just the story of a camp old queen trying to get a squeeze from a lumbering big oaf. The movie throws in the analogies with Frankenstein, the gardener's war experiences, thoughts on humanity … anything to make it look complex and thoughtful.

Sorry – you failed. *Gods and Monsters*, no matter how much window dressing is chucked at it, is just the story of an aging poof trying to get off with the staff. The addition of poor old Lynn Redgrave serving tea in the shed is nothing short of cruel.

Gone With the Wind

Scarlett suffers greatly during the American Civil War, but she only really wants to be with Ashley. And what Scarlett wants she usually gets.

Director	Victor Flemming
Writer	Sidney Howard (from Margaret Mitchell's book)
Starring	Clark Gable
	Vivien Leigh
	Leslie Howard
	Olivia de Havilland
Released	1939
Awards	Won nine Oscars, and got four further nominations and an honorary Award for William Cameron Menzies for outstanding use of colour. Vivien Leigh got the New York Film Critics Circle Award for Best Actress, and the film won the People's Choice award for Favourite All-time Motion Picture in 1989.
Box office	$390,500,000 (Worldwide)
Tagline	The most magnificent picture ever!

"The mother of all event movies…" Peter Bradshaw, *Guardian*

Come on, I didn't have a choice. It had to be in, didn't it? The opening and closing lines are perhaps the most famous in film history, the search for Scarlett legendary, and everybody over 40 knows where they were the first time they saw it. *Gone with the Wind* is a film icon. But it's rubbish!

At the end of the day you have to wonder what all the fuss was about. This is an interminably long film about a pain in the ass. You wouldn't want to spend nearly four hours on the train with Scarlett O'Hara, so why would you pay to watch her in a cinema?

If the film was actually about Scarlett and Rhett it might have been interesting, but for most of the time she's chasing after the extremely ordinary Ashley. This kills any chance of a strong driving narrative, and so we are left to meander aimlessly with a spoilt little rich girl that Gandhi would have lost patience with.

The music begins as stirring, but really starts to wear on you after a while. The Technicolor is funny in a historical sort of way, but only serves to illustrate even more that this is not reality. The last reel of the film descends into classic farce, with a member of Scarlett's family dying every couple of minutes. You end up screaming "watch yourself on those stairs," or "don't get on that horse, it's dangerous!"

So why is it considered a classic? Well, it does help to extricate the Americans from their shameful history of slavery. Our freedom-loving American cousins can simply watch *Gone With the Wind* and feel satisfied that the slaves actually liked their lives. Look how they smile and stay with their lovely owners. Can't have been that bad, could it?

Good Morning Vietnam

An armed forces DJ in Vietnam clashes with the authorities due to his unconventional style and unorthodox approach.

Director	Barry Levinson
Writer	Mitch Markowitz
Starring	Robin Williams
	Forest Whitaker
Released	1987
Awards	Two Political Film Society awards, an ASCAP award, and Robin Williams won a Golden Globe, an American Comedy Award, and was nominated for an Oscar and a BAFTA.
Box office	Worldwide US$ figure unavailable
Tagline	The wrong man. In the wrong place. At the right time.

"Williams is amazing." Gerry Shamray, *Sun Newspapers of Cleveland*, Rotten Tomatoes

"Robin Williams's best ever film." Clint Morris, Moviehole, Rotten Tomatoes

Shut up Williams! You're not funny, and your tiresome endless rants really grate on the nerves. People raved about the "comedian's" stream of consciousness raps in *Good Morning Vietnam*. I personally would have preferred the production to have invested in a script, and maybe even a script editor. I don't pay my money to hear self-satisfied lunatics rant about everything and anything – I can do that for free on any London bus.

Williams as Adrian Cronauer talks so fast and so loud in this rather inconsequential movie that he pulls the wool over everyone's eyes. Because he's saying so much we believe there must be something in there that's funny, surely. Look – that nice Forest is laughing (he does little else in the movie than laugh and be black, just to show how extra nice and caring that nice disc jockey is). And there is a certain shock factor for a while, but in the cold light of day you realize that the rambling monologues actually have no bite or traces of humour in them.

Levinson, who's no fool, throws in a starchy and ridiculous figure of authority just to exaggerate how irreverent and impertinent Cronauer is. This cynically puts us in on the battle – if we're against the Lieutenant, and we couldn't be anything else, then we're firmly in the DJ's camp.

Less successful are the crass attempts to throw in a love interest and some deeper meaning. These segments mark the worrying start of the "earnest" Williams on film, and for that reason alone the original negative should be burnt.

Good Morning Vietnam is yet another example of Hollywood allowing their audiences to be slightly subversive as a little guilty pleasure. Cronauer was, after all, only a DJ. Most of the GIs didn't listen to him because they were too busy being blown up for no apparent reason. He didn't destabilize the war effort, and would certainly never criticize the Napalm-happy forces. No, he made the odd little joke at Nixon's expense and introduced some camp characters.

And, on the evidence of this, he wasn't very funny or entertaining. Sack the DJ!

Good Will Hunting

For the first 20 years of his life, Will Hunting has called the shots. Now he's about to meet his match.

Director	Gus Van Sant
Writers	Matt Damon, Ben Affleck
Starring	Robin Williams
	Matt Damon
	Ben Affleck
Released	1997
Awards	Oscars for the screenplay and for Robin Williams (who also got a Screen Actors Guild award) and nominated for seven more. The screenplay also won a Golden Globe. The film got another 14 awards, and 27 further nominations.
Box office	$225,800,000
Tagline	Wildly charismatic. Impossibly brilliant. Totally rebellious.

"Will's relationships with his best friend, Chuckie (Affleck), and new girlfriend, Skylar (Minnie Driver), resonate with a depth that unfortunately few other movies approach. MaryAnn Johanson, Flick Filosopher

"Touching, without being sentimental, and feelgood without appearing contrived..." Nev Pierce, BBCi

Robin Williams is trying to take over this book! So for this entry we'll try to ignore his cloying and extremely cheesy performance and get to the real reason why *Good Will Hunting* fails.

This is simply an absurd film – tawdry wish-fulfilment by two young writers who managed to fool everybody. Come on – Matt Damon and Ben Affleck as a pair of rebel-rousing drunken street fighters? They hardly put the fear of God into you, do they ("did you spill my moisturiser?")? That whole concept just doesn't work. They don't look, talk or behave like a couple of kids from the wrong side of the tracks (you can swear all you like boys, but it's just not happening).

Add to that the idea that the janitor at MIT (probably the only janitor under the age of 60) is actually a maths genius who is smarter that those stuck-up preppy students. This is a premise for a teenager's fantasy, not a proper film for grown-ups. Most preposterous of a totally ridiculous film is the scene where the young janitor goes into a bar, belittles the arrogant brainiac student and wins the girl. Yeah, right – happens all the time.

Good Will Hunting is full of angst and impassioned speeches, but has no real depth or purpose. It's an immature script that should never have been made into a film in the first place. It then beggars belief that it received such adulation. Just goes to show you that miracles do happen at times; especially if Harvey Weinstein wants them to happen.

Heavenly Creatures

The intense relationship between two teenage girls starts to worry their respective families, but the girls will stop at nothing to ensure they stay in contact.

Director	Peter Jackson
Writers	Peter Jackson, Frances Walsh
Starring	Melanie Lynskey
	Kate Winslet
Released	1994
Awards	Won every award it was up for at the New Zealand Film and TV Awards (10 in total), as well as three film festival awards, two London Critics Circle Awards, and an Empire Award for Kate Winslet. Nominated for an Oscar for the screenplay.
Box office	Worldwide US$ figure unavailable
Tagline	The true story of a crime that shocked a nation.

"… Juliet and Pauline are never turned into monsters. Played with infinite sympathy, they give the impression of being drawn into a vortex in which the terms of survival dictate the harshest course of action." David Rooney, *Variety*

Oh, if only we could get into a time machine. Many would try to stop the Kennedy assassination, others maybe would try to avert tragedies such as Hitler's rise to power or the 9/11 bombings. Me? I'd probably try to close down the production of *Heavenly Creatures*. Without this pompous and frankly very silly movie we might have been spared Kate Winslet. Her smug grin and flicky hair have spoilt many a good movie, and when she does an American accent it's just bad, bad, bad. Watch *Eternal Sunshine of the Spotless Mind* (2004) to see how she can really screw up a good movie.

Also, if there was no *Heavenly Creatures* there would possibly have been no *Lord of the Rings*. Imagine what a great world that would be. Peter Jackson would still be stuck doing splatter movies and we'd have no geeks raving on about Middle Earth and the like. The world would be a much better place.

I didn't buy into the central relationship in *Heavenly Creatures* at all. Call me old fashioned, but I would have slapped the girls' legs a long time before they started knocking off family members.

Giggly, pretentious schoolgirls are not interesting, even if they do take their fantasies to the violent extreme, they are simply trying and tiresome. Jackson has been widely praised for his "sensitivity" and "reserve". Personally I think this would have been a much better film if he'd gone all out for the lesbian killer aspect. Skin, flesh and bone – that's what makes an entertaining film. Not the daydreams of a couple of silly little girls.

Get me my time machine now!

Hilary and Jackie

The life of accomplished cellist Jacqueline Du Pré as told by the sister who was always in Jackie's shadow.

Director	Anand Tucker
Writer	Frank Cottrell Boyce (from a book by Hilary and Piers du Pré)
Starring	Emily Watson
	Rachel Griffiths
	James Frain
Released	1998
Awards	Two British Independent Film Awards for Anand Tucker and Emily Watson, who also got a London Critics Circle Film Award. Nominated, among others, for two Oscars (Emily again and Rachel Griffiths) and five BAFTAs
Box office	$6,174,838 (Worldwide)
Tagline	The true story of two sisters who shared a passion, a madness and a man.

"A revelation when it allows us to see what people surrender for art, as well as why people surrender their art." Scott Renshaw, imdb Newsgroup reviews

Rumour has it that Emily Watson turned down the titular role in *Elizabeth* to appear in *Hilary and Jackie*. I do hope she had strong words with her agent afterwards.

On release we were bombarded with press comments from fellow cellist Julian Lloyd Webber complaining about the film and its "misrepresentation" of Jacqueline Du Pré. Julian, I'm sorry, you've rather missed the point (although, cleverly, you did bring out a record while doing all this press stuff). We don't care whether the film's portrayal of her is right or wrong, as long as it's entertaining. And in *Hilary and Jackie* it just wasn't.

The performances are OK, although you do get the feeling that Emily Watson relied too heavily on the cello and the illness (Du Pré suffered from multiple sclerosis, which finally killed her) and so didn't make a fully rounded character study. Rachel Griffiths does moody and intense well, and James Frain is actually quite charming as the conductor Jackie finally marries.

But the problem is we don't care. Most of us only have the slightest clue who this Jackie person was, and so wanted to be informed and entertained. And the movie failed in both areas. We don't know what made her so acclaimed, find it hard to recognize what her problems were … we never actually understand why she had sex with her sister's husband, and indeed why Hilary let her.

Everything is implied and nothing is properly developed in *Hilary and Jackie*. The device of flashing back and telling the story from another perspective adds little to the overall effect of the film, which was a whole lot of fuss about nothing.

House of Flying Daggers

An undercover policeman frees a young dancer from prison in the hope that she will lead him to a group of revolutionaries. But all is not as it seems.

Director	Yimou Zhang
Writers	Yimou Zhang, Feng Li, Bin Wang
Starring	Takeshi Kaneshiro
	Andy Lau
	Zhang Ziyi
Released	2004
Awards	Won 14 awards, often for Best Foreign film or for Best Cinematography. 34 assorted nominations including one for an Oscar.
Box office	Worldwide US$ figure unavailable

"Zhang Yimou has only just finished seducing us with his gorgeous extravaganza *Hero*. Now, almost without missing a beat in his career, he has conjured up another extraordinary, swoonworthy spectable. This martial-arts romance delivers what I can only call a narco-exotic rush…" Peter Bradshaw, *Guardian*

Why couldn't we just have had *Crouching Tiger, Hidden Dragon* (2000)? Nice movie, lovely scenes, worked well. But oh no – suddenly the world and his live-in partner were experts in "Asian cinema" (even though Asian meant from the Indian subcontinent before this), have always loved the genre .. blah, blah, blah. And lo and behold we are inundated in Far East cinema for which we were supposed to be grateful. Perish the thought that anyone would raise an objection against the films.

Well, I'm sorry, but it's time for the little man to speak up. It's got to be said sooner or later: *House of Flying Daggers* is a bit of a mess. It's not the beautiful and haunting classic that the reviewers would have you think. It's a confusing and unsatisfying piece of cinema from a part of the world that's very different from here. I don't think it's shallow to admit that this film wasn't made for us. We are not the intended audience, and shouldn't feel ashamed or underachieving if we don't get it. Every country makes their own movies, and only the very small fraction cross over or ever get seen abroad.

Without *Crouching Tiger* … neither *House of Flying Daggers* nor the director's previous effort *Hero* (2002) which was also a wee bit of a mess if truth be told, would have received so much attention or acclaim.

Chinese narrative conventions are different from the western ideas (these are people who read their books back to front don't forget). The stories don't have to make as much sense, the audiences on the whole are more interested in spectacle than plot. And so *House of Flying Daggers* twists and turns until you simply can't get your head around it. Characters change sides, double cross and go "undercover" constantly. The story continuously changes direction and alters its focus. Fine for the local audience – but this just confused, confounded, and then frustrated me. The action isn't even that good or original, leaving us with an annoying and untidy film.

House of Sand and Fog

A woman is evicted from her house, but embarks on a bitter and violent feud with the home's new owners.

Director	Vadim Perelman
Writers	Vadim Perelman, Shawn Otto (from Andre Dubus III's book)
Starring	Jennifer Connelly
	Ben Kingsley
	Ron Eldard
Released	2003
Awards	Won six awards from various Film Critics Circles, and an Independent Spirit Award. Nominated for three Oscars and a Golden Globe, among others.
Box office	Worldwide US$ figure unavailable.
Tagline	Some dreams can't be shared.

"Not easy to sit through, but it has something worthwhile to communicate and strong actors who go all out to communicate it." Jeffrey Chen, *Window to the Movies*

"… mostly it's a vigorous and bracingly acted melodrama spun off from a situation that's pure human-thriller catnip." Owen Gleiberman, *Entertainment Weekly*

Take a book adaptation, stick in the man who gave us *Gandhi* (1982) and soppy Oscar-winner Jennifer Connelly, and you can't go wrong. Hmmm.

I cannot believe the amount of people who bought into this drab and uninteresting film. Ironically the movie is built on sand – we're supposed to feel sorry for the lead, who has been evicted mainly because she hasn't opened her mail for months. I'm sorry, call me hard-hearted, there's not a whole load of sympathy coming from me here. The story tries to imply that this is because of some form of mental breakdown (and alcohol dependence). But still ... tough. She wasn't hoodwinked out of her home, there was no secret agenda. She lost it because she screwed up. Kinda sad, but hey – what can you do?

And it's only a house. Why should we care? She hasn't lost a leg, or a lover. She's been bumped out of her home because she's too crap to open her mail. Sorry, all chances of emotional and intellectual engagement gone completely.

Add to that the usual hammy Ben Kingsley performance (motto: never underact when you can go over the top) and the excruciatingly boring Connelly and you've got a waste of a movie. A bitter feud between an aging ex-army immigrant and a sad lonely alcoholic is not a strong enough premise to get the audience licking their lips.

This is not a lyrical or beautiful movie, and the only real tragedy is the waste of the two hours I spent watching it.

Ice Age

Four prehistoric animals embark on a task of returning a human child to his father before the ice age sets in.

Directors	Chris Wedge and Carlos Saldanha
Writers	Michael J. Wilson, Michael Berg, Peter Ackerman, et al
Starring	Ray Romano
	John Leguizamo
	Denis Leary
	Goran Visnjic
Released	2002
Awards	Won a BMI Film Music Award, a Bogey Award, and two awards from Film Critics Circles in Italy and Kansas. Nominated for an Oscar, and seven Annie awards among its 22 nominations.
Box office	$378,300,000
Tagline	The coolest event in 16,000 years.

"… consistently entertaining and delightful throughout." Jane Crowther, BBCi

"The whole plot is based heavily on evolutionary theory with the obvious funny looking animals – almost like 'unevolved' versions of our present-day animals. But Creationists need not worry about any heavy indoctrination… this movie provides good clean humor and dialogue." Robin Tan, *Christian Spotlight on the Movies*

Ice Age is hugely popular, it spawned a really successful sequel, and it is loved across the globe. It has cute characters, strong animation and a decent cast of voices (including Jack Black and Cedric the Entertainer).

So why, if you'll excuse the pun, does it leave me cold? I think it's a mixture of those lovely people at Fox Animation simply following a formula, with little deviation or imagination shown, and the fact that family fare has moved on.

You can't watch the likes of *Shrek* (2001) or *Toy Story* (1995) and then still be entertained by *Ice Age*. We've been spoiled. And once you move on it's hard to sit through the old stuff again. For Heaven's sake, *Jungle Book* (1967) doesn't look all that good now.

The artistic bar has been raised, and *Ice Age* sadly fell under it. All the main strengths of animated product are there – strong motivations, different well-rounded characters, a very explicit purpose to the story, etc. But where are the edgy wise-cracks and the knowing winks to the audience? Where's the humour that works on different levels and the post-ironic swipes at other films and crazes?

Ice Age is firmly stuck in the ice age. There's no pizzazz or balls about the project. The film has made an enormous amount of money, but mostly from kids going back and back (thanks mostly to the huge marketing spend). It is not a film that adults can take to. You could never say that it's actually bad, but it's 10 years behind its time. Coming from the global brand that makes *The Simpsons* it is very odd that the film is so reactive and derivative – and so it has to go into the list of overrated films for that alone.

In the Cut

A professor of English falls headfirst into a steamy relationship with a homicide detective, but the more she learns about men the more she fears them.

Director	Jane Campion
Writers	Jane Campion, Susanna Moore (from Susanna Moore's book)
Starring	Jennifer Jason Leigh
	Meg Ryan
Released	2003
Awards	Won a Golden Tripod from the Australian Cinematographers Society and nominated for a Golden Frog and a Golden Spike from Camerimage and the Valladolid International Film Festival respectively.
Box office	Worldwide US$ figure unavailable
Tagline	Everything you know about desire is dead wrong.

"It's an art movie for the masses." David Sterritt, *Christian Science Monitor*

"An honest look at sexuality as perceived by women." Dennis Schwartz, Ozus' World Movie Reviews

Good girl Meg Ryan. What better way to be taken more seriously than simply get your kit off? Why didn't we all think of it?

This movie split even the most pretentious of the chattering classes (derided by some, but lauded by others and even chosen as Opening Night Film for The London Film Festival that year). But it is included in the list as a warning to anyone who gets fooled into considering a viewing. Stay away – *In the Cut* is so bad that it could affect your health.

I'm being serious, this is a film that will make you grind your teeth and perhaps even start to beat yourself up to get away from the dreadfulness of it. It's not erotic, it's not thrilling, it lacks intelligence and says nothing. It's not even so bad that it is funny (a bizarre fellatio scene using a prosthetic penis that looked more like a red water balloon being the only giggle).

Meg Ryan looks odd, acts odd, gets naked (which nobody wants to see dear) and generally flounces around suspecting everyone of being the serial killer (especially the black student who she takes on for no apparent reason). Mark Ruffalo manages to give one of the worst performances ever seen outside amateur dramatics, and Jennifer Jason Leigh seems to fall onto the set from another movie without noticing. And the less said about poor old Kevin Bacon the better.

Pretensions abound, including the main character writing sayings on post-its and slapping them all over her house (please tell me no one really does that). The much lauded sex scenes are less believable than Meg's false orgasm in *When Harry Met Sally* (1989), and the denouement is much more of a relief than a surprise.

Be wary. There are people out there that like *In the Cut*, and tell you that you're obviously too uptight/stupid/insensitive (delete as appropriate) to appreciate it. Walk away from these people slowly, without breaking eye contact, and then phone the social services to come and get them.

The King

Just discharged from the Navy Elvis travels to the deep south to meet the father he never knew.

Director	James Marsh
Writers	James Marsh, Milo Addica
Starring	Gael Garcia Bernal
	William Hurt
Released	2005
Awards	Won the American Independents Award at the Philadelphia Film Festival. No other nominations.
Box office	Worldwide US$ figure unavailable
Tagline	The devil made me do it.

"Marsh and Addica refrain from trumping up the menace; instead, *The King* draws its feeling of dread from a profound and pervasive ambivalence." Carina Chocano, *Los Angeles Times*

"… a fascinating psychological drama that puts the boot into the delusions, hypocrisy and cruelty of American Christian fundamentalism." Philip French, *Observer*

You do wonder how some films ever get made, and *The King* (with its incredibly poor script) is certainly one of them. But then to get a topline cast including Gael Garcia Bernal and William Hurt attached is quite an achievement. What a shame all that effort was wasted.

The problem isn't with the premise, which although a tad hackneyed could have been interesting. Where the film goes wrong is the lack of investment into the characters. And so, when the young girl discovers that she has been having sex with her half-brother, the whole audience laughs rather than empathizes with her. We never get to know any of the characters, and so really don't care about them.

The King is a nasty film which blithely uses violence without any discussion of cause and effect. Similarly the sex scenes have an unhealthy tinge of paedophilia about them. A lack of emotion pervades the full film, which was probably on purpose – but because everything is so underplayed it fails to engage our sense or emotions.

It is a mystery how *The King* became a film festivals' favourite. It is a soulless and empty movie that is unsure what it wants to say or do. We never really learn the protagonist's back story or his reasoning, so the piece completely lacks direction.

Stay away, or you will feel positively depressed, down and dirty afterwards (and not in a good way).

Ladies in Lavender

Two sisters in a small coastal community discover a strange foreigner washed up on the beach; as they care for him they must deal with the locals' suspicions and their own sibling rivalry.

Director	Charles Dance
Writer	Charles Dance (from William J. Locke's short story)
Starring	Judi Dench
	Maggie Smith
	Natascha McElhone
Released	2004
Awards	Judi Dench and Maggie Smith were both nominated for Best Actress Audience Awards at the European Film Awards.
Box office	Worldwide US$ figure unavailable
Tagline	They saved a stranger from the sea and in return he stole their hearts.

"… characteristically excellent work from Smith (all suppression and stoicism) and Dench (exuding unfulfilled yearning)." Philip French, Guardian Unlimited

"This is the most impressive directing debut by a 'name' British actor in a long, long time." William Arnold, *Seattle Post-Intelligencer*

"The film is a small study in letting go." Michael O'Sullivan, *Washington Post*

Film making by numbers for old people. Speaking generally, people over the age of 45 (who do make up nearly half the population now) only go to the cinema once or twice a year. In recent years both *Mrs. Henderson Presents* (2005) and *Calendar Girls* (2003) have managed to snaffle this market. And in 2004 it was the turn of *Ladies in Lavender,* actor Charles Dance's directorial debut.

And golly gosh, if it isn't formulaic cynical rubbish! Don't worry about proper script or decent photography; just get two dames to play the leading roles. It means that you don't really have to direct them, just let them get on with hamming it up; and no one's going to criticize you with two acting treasures in the lead.

So we get Maggie Smith and Judi Dench obviously having a ball at our expense. No control seems to have been put on them so they go hell for leather to steal each scene. The story, where there is one, is predictable, old fashioned and cutesy. Everything the audience wants. Except that, even though they're getting a wee bit senile, and really should go and support their local cinema more, this audience deserves more than oldie autopilot for their entertainment. Proper screen actress Natascha McElhone shows the two ennobled luvvies how it should be done, and you must feel sorry for her (in fact, over the years McElhone has proved what a great film actress she is, but has received scant praise).

Everyone else involved in this shoddy exercise in robbing the old should just feel very guilty. OK, I know cinemas hate the crinklies coming in – they can't eat popcorn because it gets under their dentures, and they'd rather have a nice cup of tea to a Coke Zero, but we'll all be like that some day. And I hope I'm not watching half-assed fare like this when I am!

Last Tango in Paris

A middle-aged businessman and a young woman embark on a relationship that is purely sexual, to the point where they do not even learn each other's names.

Director	Bernardo Bertolucci
Writers	Bernardo Bertolucci, Franco Arcalli, Agnès Varda
Starring	Marlon Brando
	Maria Schneider
Released	1972
Awards	Bertolucci won a Silver Ribbon from the Italian National Syndicate of Film Journalists, and Marlon Brando won two awards from US Film Critic Societies. Maria Schneider won a Special David at the David di Donatello Awards. The film won a Golden Screen in Germany. Nominated for two Oscars (Bertolucci and Brando), a BAFTA (Brando), and two Golden Globes (Bertolucci and the film).
Box office	Worldwide US$ figure unavailable

"Although pornography documents the impersonal mechanics of sex, few serious films challenge actors to explore its human dimensions; isn't it remarkable that no film since 1972 has been more sexually intimate, revealing, honest and transgressive than *Last Tango?*" Roger Ebert, *Chicago Sun-Times*

After seeing this you'll never talk about buttering up the boss again. In fact it's so pretentious and dull that you might never talk again.

Those expecting sensual charge or hidden meaning will be disappointed by a film with a reputation that far surpasses its quality. Lots of arty excuses were made for *Last Tango* … at the time (it is about people taking refuge in sex, it is about America's relationship with Europe etc.). Bah humbug. Bertolucci has always been a bit of a dirty old man (have a look at some of the early, quite unnecessary, scenes in *The Sheltering Sky* (1990)) and here was his opportunity to film a bit of rumpy-pumpy without even having to build a story around it. Similarly old Brando probably saw it as his last opportunity for some action before he became too obese to copulate with anything smaller than a sperm whale (is that where they get their name I wonder?).

The whole film is more reminiscent of a nature film than a feature film. Our rutting leads basically grunt and sweat their way through the film without actually showing us anything except for their bodies – and to me that just isn't enough. I may be naïve, but I didn't even know what he was doing with the knob of butter (yes, I know).

This is a typical example of a movie that the critics put up on a pedestal specifically because the authorities had tried to ban it. If there hadn't been such a hoo-ha at the time it would just have gone down as another Brando folly (raging clerics please take note). You may have heard of it, but don't bother seeing it. The only good news is that the original Italian cut was 250 minutes, so at least we were spared that.

However, should they wish to remake it the product placement people might want to talk to the company behind "I Can't Believe It's Not Butter"!

The Man Who Knew Too Much

A couple's young son is kidnapped when they overhear details of a political assassination, and they must travel to London to find him.

Director	Alfred Hitchcock
Writers	Charles Bennett, D. B. Wyndham-Lewis, John Michael Hayes
Starring	James Stewart
	Doris Day
Released	1956
Awards	Won an Oscar for the Best Song ("Whatever Will Be, Will Be (Que Sera, Sera)", and an ASCAP award in 1990 for the Most Performed Feature Film Standards. Alfred Hitchcock was nominated for a Golden Palm at Cannes and a Directors Guild of America award for Outstanding Directorial Achievement in Motion Pictures.
Box office	Worldwide US$ figure unavailable
Tagline	A little knowledge can be a deadly thing!

"Compared to its 1934 predecessor, this version is more technically accomplished and suspenseful than the action-oriented original.…There's no doubt that the later version of *The Man Who Knew Too Much* is the product of a master in his prime." Bob Aulert, culturevulture.net

Put a Hitch movie in the book? Oh my God, there will be demonstrations. Especially one that stars James Stewart and Doris Day too. It's sacrilege.

Let this be a lesson to you, don't just rely on a good director always coming up with the goods. Even the master himself can slip up. And the strange thing is that this was Hitchcock's second stab at *The Man Who Knew Too Much*. He wasn't happy with his 1934 version of the film (which he described as the work of an amateur) so decided to remake it (please take note all those constantly sniping that there are too many remakes today).

And what a disappointment it turns out to be. The idea is fine, the core story is fine, but the film really lacks all the director's usual touches – tension, intelligence and razor-sharp pacing. Instead *The Man Who Knew Too Much* kinda plods along as they traipse through Morocco and London, with hardly a tourist landmark unvisited.

The photography is horrible, the plot twists have no resonance, and strangely there is no spark at all between Day and Stewart (you would have thought that after all that time with Rock Hudson she would have been grateful!).

Still, at least we get a nice little rendition of "Que Sera Sera" (which you don't really expect in a supposedly taut thriller), but you just want a little bit more from Hitchcock.

Marie Antoinette

The life and loves of the Hapsburg princess who embarks on a sexless marriage with the French Dauphin, is crowned queen at 19 and then beheaded years later.

Director	Sofia Coppola
Writer	Sofia Coppola
Starring	Kirsten Dunst
	Jason Schwartzman
	Judy Davis
	Rip Torn
Released	2006
Awards	At the time of writing, the movie was not yet on general release but had picked up the Cinema Prize of the French National Education System at Cannes and been nominated for the Golden Palm.
Box office	Worldwide US$ figure unavailable
Tagline	Let them eat cake.

"A demanding film…. The principal ambition is to lose us through flirting, like the heroine, in order to penetrate, with staggering empathy, an intimate universe severed from the moment – a universe of intoxication, frivolities and satiety."
Frédéric Flament, *Plume Noire*

I never thought that I would get sick of looking at Kirsten Dunst. But there is so little in this movie – the word flimsy positively oversells it – that all you can do is gaze at the loveliness of the young actress. And after a while (over two hours) even her inestimable charms start to wear thin.

I like Sofia Coppola's work so far (well … as a director. We'll quickly gloss over her acting in *Godfather III* (1990)). And I can see what she's trying to do here – the object really is to portray how shallow and insignificant the lifestyle of Marie Antoinette really was. But by succeeding Coppola has made the filmic equivalent of a profiterole. It's ever so light, ever so sweet, but has no substance and nothing to remember.

It looks marvellous, the scenery and the costumes are top notch, but says absolutely nothing. We learn nothing about the leading character, nothing about the history of the day, nothing about the social unrest or even of the workings of court. *Marie Antoinette* takes insignificance to a new level. When one of Marie's children dies this is dramatized on screen by the infant being simply eradicated from a painting – no scenes of distraught young girl becoming a woman, no clue into how this shaped the rest of her life. Nothing.

And that's disappointing to say the least. I expected better, much better, from an inspired and original director and one of the best young screen actresses currently working. But they've got away with it. Obviously divisive when shown at the Cannes Film Festival, those who loved it shouted from the heavens about its apparent merits (yes, we know it looks beautiful, but some of us want more). The utilization of pop music for some scenes is not only unoriginal (step forward *A Knight's Tale* (2001)), but also totally overused.

It's all such a shame because it was so avoidable, but this little puff pastry should be avoided at all costs. I'd rather eat cake.

Mary Poppins

A mysterious and quite magical nanny comes to look after two unhappy children, and she manages to give them back their childhoods.

Director	Robert Stevenson
Writers	Bill Walsh, Don Da Gradi (from the books by P. L. Travers)
Starring	Julie Andrews
	Dick Van Dyke
	David Tomlinson
	Glynis Johns
Released	1964
Awards	Won five Oscars and nominated for eight more. Won four Golden Laurels. Julie Andrews won a BAFTA and a Golden Globe. The score won a Grammy, and the screenwriters won a Writers Guild of America award.
Box office	Worldwide US$ figure unavailable
Tagline	It's supercalifragilisticexpialidocious!

"Even better than you remember, better than anyone could have hoped, better than almost any other movie of its kind."
Nick Davis, Nick's Flick Picks, Rotten Tomatoes

It's an iconic movie, but it has to be said – Mary Poppins isn't actually very good. Or let's qualify that for the sake of the book. It's overrated because it could have been so much more. Read the books, go see the stage show, and you will realize that this is a great and inspiring musical.

But Disney got hold of it and covered it with their very own spoonful of sugar, to make it palatable to the great American public. The essence of *Mary Poppins* is actually quite subversive and edgy. The stories tell you to express yourself, have a bit of fun, don't get too caught up in life's boring detail – use your imagination. All great mottos for children to follow.

Instead the company of the mouse employed the far-too-prim and prissy Julie Andrews to be the mystical, almost white-witch like Poppins – who might as well have blown in from Surbiton than somewhere magical. The songs and the special effects took over in importance from the core message and enchantment in the story and hey presto, they get a blockbuster hit that won't teach the kids to overstretch themselves.

OK, we know that Dick Van Dyke's (why name your son Dick Van? There must be a reason) accent really is terrible. But to be honest he's probably the best thing in the film. It is his exuberance and pratfalls that keep it going while Andrews whines and tuts like a virgin schoolmarm.

The mix of animation and live action is good, some of the songs aren't bad at all, but *Mary Poppins* could have been so much better – a real groundbreaking inspiration to a generation of kids instead of just a pleasant and unchallenging Disney film.

Match Point

A tennis teacher looks ahead to a life of wealth and influence by becoming engaged, but then falls for a struggling actress. Will his overriding passion allow him to give up the lifestyle he has only just acquired?

Director	Woody Allen
Writer	Woody Allen
Starring	Jonathan Rhys Meyers
	Alexander Armstrong
	Scarlett Johansson
	Paul Kaye
Released	2005
Awards	Won four awards as Best Foreign or European Film and a Golden Trailer for Best Thriller. Among the ten nominations were an Oscar, a César, and four Golden Globes.
Box office	Worldwide US$ figure unavailable
Tagline	Passion Temptation Obsession.

"[The film is] suffused with a Fitzgeraldian glow of bittersweet romance and ruefulness among the elite." Gene Seymour, *Newsday*

"[Allen's] most satisfying film in more than a decade…" A. O. Scott, *New York Times*

Some things are so remarkable to become almost unbelievable: a bird migrating to exactly the same place each year, the pyramids, Cliff Richard still being single ... but above them all, the most surprising thing ever, is that *Match Point* got good reviews.

This is a movie so horrendously hackneyed and stupid that to even write about it causes shivers up and down my spine. Yet some people, who get paid for their opinion and presumably see quite a few movies, actually acclaimed it. Words fail me ... not for long, of course.

Woody Allen is like the little old man in the pub who collects the glasses. His hands can no longer grab because of rheumatism, and he's so slow that he's not actually helping; but hey, he's been doing it for years, and some people remember him when he could do the job properly, so you might as well let him get on with it. Similarly the film world lets Allen get on and make his movies. He's doing no harm, saves him being cooped inside with the kids ... no one's going to watch any of the films now, but it keeps him out of mischief. Arguably he has not made a decent film since *Annie Hall* (1977), and even his biggest fans would be stretched to give compliments for any of his work in the 21st century.

But then *Match Point* comes out and people are singing his praises again. Please don't be fooled. Well over half the movie is just excruciating – the kind of vision Americans used to have about London before they started traveling (everyone has a country mansion and drops in at the opera a couple of times a week). The performances are woeful – with Jonathan Rhys Meyers constantly looking as if he can't remember his next line (or maybe he just can't believe it) and Scarlett Johansson trying desperately to be some form of Diana Dors character. It is also a little too creepy the way Woody lingers the camera on Scarlett the whole time – yuck.

Then in the second half Allen tries to throw in some sort of storyline, which really kills the film completely. Time we just pretended to put film in the camera for Woody Allen, it will make things much easier all round.

The Matrix

In the not too distant future a young man discovers that reality is an illusion and the human race is being kept captive.

Directors	The Wachowski Brothers
Writers	Andy Wachowski, Larry Wachowski
Starring	Keanu Reeves
	Laurence Fishburne
	Carrie-Anne Moss
	Hugo Weaving
Released	1999
Awards	Among the 32 awards and 35 nominations it received, the film got four Oscars for Sound and Visual Effects, Sound and Editing. Two BAFTAs, for visual effects and sound, and nominated for three more technical awards. Awards for the actors came from the Blockbuster Entertainment Awards and Empire Awards.
Box office	$456,300,000 (Worldwide)
Tagline	What is the Matrix?

"The most influential action movie since *Star Wars*." Steven D. Greydanus, *Decent Films Guide*

"*The Matrix* is a benchmark in modern action movies, both plot wise and visually it was above the level of anything seen before." Genesis, ScifiWatch

What is it about *The Matrix*? It stirs the emotions. I've got a friend who named his child Neo, some that say it changed their lives, and others that hate it with a positive vengeance (including a certain film executive who positively begged me to put the film in).

I have to say that I can't see why it has such an effect on people, and that's why it undoubtedly deserves a berth in the 101 most overrated.

Calm down people – it's a nothing film, a piece of stuff and nonsense. The whole premise is fairly messy and silly (if you disagree with the one-line synopsis you try better) – the human race is quite happy thinking they're in the 20th century, so what's the problem?

The rules and storyline get more and more complex as you go along so you really should just give up. It's really not worth it to suss out exactly what's happening. The much lauded action and photography are actually not that special. Yes, nice idea to stop someone half-way through a jump and spin the camera round. But once it's done, it's done. There's no point in the Wachowski brothers doing it again and again, because the more you use the fairly simplistic trick the less impact it has.

As with most genre flicks, our friends with the computers have taken over this film and given it mythical proportions – is Neo Christ? Does it explain our existence? Does it hell as like. It's a piece of fluff that got lost up its own bottom.

The sequels would probably be in here too, except that you need to watch the first one again before taking on the others and I simply couldn't be bothered. It's not the best film in the world, it's not the worst in the world, it's simply unremarkable (and no, my little geeky friends, there's not a conspiracy making me say this).

The Mission

A Spanish priest, who has converted a tribe of South American natives, now has to protect them against Portuguese slavers.

Director	Roland Joffe
Writer	Robert Bolt
Starring	Robert De Niro
	Jeremy Irons
	Ray McAnally
	Aidan Quinn
Released	1986
Awards	An Oscar for Best Cinematography, and nominated for six more. Three BAFTAs, and nominated for eight more, two Golden Globes and three more nominations, and the Golden Palm and the Technical Grand Prize at Cannes as well as assorted other prizes and nominations.
Box office	Worldwide US$ figure unavailable

"*The Mission* effectively dramatizes yet another chapter in the ruthless European quest of the Americas. It'll make you hate the whole of western civilization with every fiber of your being."
Rita Kempley, *Washington Post*

One minute you're up, the next you're down. The film industry is a cruel business. And the best example is Roland Joffe. After the rather brilliant *The Killing Fields* (1984) he's let loose with a decent budget and an all-star cast (including Robert De Niro). So he bored the pants off us, and ended up being one of the uncredited directors on *Super Mario Bros* (1993).

Where did it all go wrong? Probably by taking himself too seriously. There is no light hand at work at *The Mission*. Strangely acclaimed as a masterpiece by many, the truth of the matter is that it is a rambling, shambolic story about a bunch of little foreigners that we don't really care for.

Joffe tries to imbue the film with modern resonance, and desperately tries to engage us in the injustice of the story (which I presume is true-life as no one could be quite so boring as to make it up). A droning Morricone score does nothing to relieve the tedium as Jeremy Irons tries desperately to do the right thing, in the face of those fiendish Portuguese. That just about sums it up – who has ever really had strong feelings about the Portuguese? Even when they beat England at football (again and again) the tabloids can think of very little to throw at them.

The Mission looks spectacular, but once you've seen one rainforest you've seen the lot (and John Boorman did do it so much better).

Sorry Roland, life really is too short to be bothered trying to get into *The Mission*, and following the earnest but boring events.

Monster's Ball

A prison guard from a racist family re-evaluates his life when he falls in love with a black woman (whose husband he has executed).

Director	Mark Forster
Writers	Milo Addica, Will Rokos
Starring	Billy Bob Thornton
	Halle Berry
Released	2001
Awards	One Oscar (Halle Berry) and one nomination for the screenplay. She also won a Silver Berlin Bear, and awards from Black Reel, the National Board of Review and the Screen Actors Guild. Billy Bob Thornton won awards from the Florida Film Critics Circle and the National Board of Review, and the screenplay won a Golden Satellite Award.
Box office	Worldwide US$ figure unavailable
Tagline	A lifetime of change can happen in a single moment.

"The performances ... are riveting. As Hank, Thornton is so understated and assured, he pulls you in... And Berry, whose acting skills have rarely enjoyed the showcasing they deserve, certainly makes her stamp here." Desson Howe, *Washington Post*

When picking up her totally undeserved Oscar for *Monster's Ball*, Halle Berry was quoted as saying that it was such a great step forward for multi-culturalism as her character didn't need to be black. Ermmm, think you were missing the point a wee bit there dear. A racist prison guard going off with a white woman doesn't give us much of a story really.

Mind you, as it is *Monster's Ball* wasn't much of a story anyway. But suddenly it was the soup of the day. It never ceases to amaze me how these things take off, but for a while you were a social leper if you hadn't seen and enjoyed the film.

Well I managed the former, but trust me – there's little to enjoy. *Monster's Ball* has no subtlety or underlying intelligence, it's a broad and extremely obvious attempt to be vaguely controversial without actually saying anything or investigating any real part of the human psyche. It pretends to be serious-minded and mature, but it's little more than a weak attempt at shock value with lots of gratuitous sex, violence and racism to stir the soul.

And I hate to mention it – but I just do not get Halle Berry. Apart from the fact that she didn't realize that her role here was for a black woman, and it's not her fault that she's a wee bit dim, I just don't find her talented or particularly sexy.

Billy Bob Thornton was watchable as ever, but dragged down by sloppy direction (just point the camera at them and see what happens seems to be the order of the day) and overworked clichés. *Monster's Ball* is no cinematic treat.

Mulholland Drive

A young actress arrives in LA seeking fame and fortune, but instead becomes embroiled in a weird mystery.

Director	David Lynch
Writer	David Lynch
Starring	Naomi Watts
	Laura Elena Harring
	Ann Miller
Released	2001
Awards	Won 30 awards in total, including Best Director at Cannes, a César for Best Foreign Film, a BAFTA for Best Editing and a host of awards from Film Critics Circles. It was nominated for a Best Director Oscar and the Golden Palm at Cannes amongst a total of 30 nominations.
Box office	Worldwide US$ figure unavailable
Tagline	A love story in the city of dreams.

"… it has an extraordinary atmosphere, a loopy, spacey persuasiveness; it has a lush visual invention, a yearning score by Angelo Badalementi, and a genial cameo by Hollywood veteran Ann Miller. Above all, it has a top-notch, all-stops-out, bells-ringing, lights-flashing star performance from Naomi Watts…" Peter Bradshaw, *Guardian*

This is perhaps the best first half to a movie I've ever seen. It has style, wit, intrigue, glamour. I was sitting there loving it; thinking that after the very good *The Straight Story* (1999), Lynch has finally made the film we all knew he was capable of. And then he takes a rush of blood to the head and screws the whole thing up. David, David, why did you desert me?

After skilfully setting up *Mulholland Drive* as a mystery thriller, he decided to throw the whole thing up in the air and see where the pieces landed. So the second half was a completely different, and extremely inaccessible load of old tosh.

Lots of people enthused over it, and surmised what actually happened or what Lynch's vision was. But the plain truth is obviously that he pressed the self-destruct button. Not only do I not know what the second half is all about; I don't really care. I came out of the cinema feeling that I was the victim of a cruel practical joke. Lynch had me on a lead, showing me what he was capable of, and then basically laughed in my face: "Ha, ha – see what I can do? Well I'm not going to!"

Mind you, I feel a little better knowing that he's having an even bigger joke on the ostentatious and mouthy "cinephiles" who loudly proclaimed that they knew exactly what he was doing with the film. I don't think he had a clue, and basically lost his nerve. Better to be misunderstood than attempt genius and fail.

My Beautiful Laundrette

A white skinhead and a young Asian entrepreneur go into business together running a glamorous laundromat, and soon become lovers.

Director	Stephen Frears
Writer	Hanif Kureishi
Starring	Saeed Jaffrey
	Roshan Seth
	Daniel Day Lewis
Released	1985
Awards	Won five awards, two for the screenplay, two for Daniel Day Lewis and one as Best Film from the Evening Standard. The screenplay was nominated for an Oscar and a BAFTA. Saeed Jaffrey was nominated for a BAFTA.
Box office	Worldwide US$ figure unavailable

"The movie is not concerned with plot, but with giving us a feeling for the society its characters inhabit. Modern Britain is a study in contrasts, between rich and poor, between upper and lower classes, between native British and the various immigrant groups – some of which, such as the Pakistanis, have started to prosper." Roger Ebert, *Chicago Sun-Times*

OK so we have race, homosexuality, class friction, politics … no kitchen sink, but everything else is chucked in by Frears to see what will work. *My Beautiful Laundrette* is shallow and opportunistic – get as many trendy topics into one film and anyone who doesn't like Thatcher and the yuppies will foolishly follow. And follow they did.

My Beautiful Laundrette got heaped with praise despite the fact that it's poorly scripted, has little story and the performances are terrible. Social realism? This film is set in Toytown. It has no bearing to what was happening in Britain at the time (except, of course, for the millions of National Front skinheads who were falling in love with Pakistani men and opening washing facilities) and has no real edge to it.

Everybody remembers the "sensual" scenes (urgh, not for me I'm afraid) and how lovely the laundrette was (although anyone who has ever had to lug their washing down to one of these places will tell you that they could never be anything more than an invention by Dante). Most forget that over half of this film is boring twaddle about the role of Asians in England, family loyalty etc.

This is because the film was written by Hanif Kureishi, a man who has blighted the British film industry for many years and only gets away with it because there's a regular amount of naughtiness thrown in. You see this name on the title please run in the other direction (especially if the title is *Intimacy* (2001)); you see his name and Frears's name together on the poster (don't even mention *Sammy and Rosie Get Laid* (1987)) please employ Daniel Day Lewis to burn down the cinema.

Nine ½ Weeks

An art gallery attendant becomes involved in a deeply sexual relationship with a man she knows nothing about.

Director	Adrian Lyne
Writers	Sarah Kernochan, Zalman King, Patricia Louisianna Knop (from Elizabeth McNeill's book)
Starring	Mickey Rourke
	Kim Basinger
Released	1986
Awards	Nominated for three Razzies: Worst Actress, Worst Original Song, Worst Screenplay
Box office	Worldwide US$ figure unavailable
Tagline	They broke every rule.

"… already notorious as the most explicitly sexual big-budget film since *Last Tango in Paris*. I went expecting erotic brinksmanship … and came away surprised by how thoughtful the movie is, how clearly it sees what really happens between its characters. That's not to say the movie isn't sexy." Roger Ebert, *Chicago Sun-Times*

Oh, what's the point? Just turn back some pages and read the comments on *Last Tango in Paris*. It's the same film with a slightly better soundtrack and a wider range of foodstuffs (strange how fat both Brando and Rourke got after doing these movies).

It's an extremely cynical movie as Lyne merely takes Bertolucci's idea (which wasn't really that interesting anyway), gets a soft porn hack to pen a new version (Zalman King, who was also one of the millions of producers) and hey presto, a film about modern issues and the human condition … that men could also enjoy viewing alone.

This is just another great example of the pretentious getting horny and not wanting *Lesbian Lipsmackers 4* on their DVD rental record. And so they invent deeper meanings and interesting themes (see "I only buy it for the articles" as other excuses).

Nine ½ Weeks is, and always was, a fairly tacky and not very arousing movie. It all but ended Mickey Rourke's career (not helped by the fact that he did the sequel, *Wild Orchid* (1990) – Mickey, that boxing really affected your judgment) and probably caused blindness in a few.

In one way this film is totally symptomatic of the 1980s – the fact that so many people were deluded (mostly because they wanted to be) to make so much money for little time and effort probably does sum up the decade more than any other film (even *Wall Street* (1987)). But for my own sanity I'll go for *Ferris Bueller's Day Off* (1986) every time thank you.

The Pianist

A brilliant Jewish pianist tries to escape the concentration camps and hides out in the Warsaw ghetto.

Director	Roman Polanski
Writer	Ronald Harwood, (from Wladyslaw Szpilman's book)
Starring	Adrien Brody
	Thomas Kretschmann
	Frank Finlay
	Maureen Lipman
Released	2002
Awards	Oscars for Best Actor, Best Director, Best Writing Oscar nominated for Best Picture, Cinematography, Editing, Costume Design. Also won best picture and director at the BAFTAs, The Golden Palm at Cannes, best nearly everything at the Césars, and even more at the Polish Film Awards.
Box office	Worldwide US$ figure unavailable
Tagline	Music was his passion. Survival was his masterpiece.

"Polanski's direction, his use of pause and nuance, is masterful."
Roger Ebert, *Chicago Sun-Times*

"Nothing can detract from the film as a portrait of hell so shattering it's impossible to shake." Peter Travers, *Rolling Stone*

OK – so I grant you that the holocaust was a truly terrible period in world history. But does that really give people the licence to make poor films about the era and not receive a rotten tomato or two? To be honest, the subject matter is so emotional and so full of the basest human emotions, that you would actually think it impossible to make a bad film about it.

Schindler's List (1993), *Life is Beautiful* (1997), even the television mini-series – all good drama. But *The Pianist*? It's little more than "holocaust by numbers." Every moment in the film is crudely and cynically stretched out for emotional response. The sad end product though is cold and uninvolving (as is most of Polanski's work since the death of Sharon Tate), with the stock scenes (brutal German shooting people for no reason) having no real impact at all.

Adrien Brody is dull, dull, dull in the lead role (he doesn't even play the piano for God's sake!). Yes, we've all heard about how much weight he'd lost for the part – but as Olivier once famously said to Dustin Hoffman: "Have you ever tried acting dear boy?" The mawkish finale, for those that manage to stay awake (the film drags worse than a wet cigarette) sums up the hamfisted manipulation perfectly. Cry? I was elated to get out.

What makes this worse is that Polanski's own family died in the Holocaust, and he just managed to escape. But instead of using these experiences to make a heartfelt film, he wears them as a badge of honour so nobody will doubt his story or criticize his movie.

The Piano

A mother (who doesn't speak) is sent to New Zealand with her young daughter to marry someone she has never met.

Director	Jane Campion
Writer	Jane Campion
Starring	Holly Hunter
	Harvey Keitel
	Sam Neill
	Anna Paquin
Released	1993
Awards	Holly Hunter, Jane Campion and Anna Paquin all won Oscars, and the film got another five nominations there. It won three BAFTAs, and was nominated for seven more. Won the Golden Palm and Best Actress at Cannes, a César for Best Foreign Film, a Golden Globe for Holly Hunter and five more nominations, etc., etc. In total it won 52 prizes.
Box office	Worldwide US$ figure unavailable

"Ada's playing is a siren's song, and though her husband seems deaf to its call, Baines, the more natural, elemental creature, responds immediately … the scenes between Hunter and Keitel are as sexually charged as any in recent years." Hal Hinson, *Washington Post*

"*The Piano* confirms Campion as a major talent, an uncompromising filmmaker with a very personal and specific vision." David Stratton, *Variety*

Jane bloody Campion again. The queen of pretension! You could win a Nobel Prize by just stealing her clapperboard away from her. And *The Piano* is her pièce de résistance – not because it is her worst (you'd have to try really hard to beat *In the Cut* (2003), although *Sweetie* (1989) comes damned close), but because so many people were suckered by it.

Her lead is mute, or perhaps refuses to speak because she has no say in her own life (anybody going to be sick yet?). The one piece of beauty in her life is this piano, which she brings with her to the new land on a rickety boat (a scene straight out of Monty Python). We are supposed to feel the mood and emotions through the tunes that Holly Hunter chops out on the old "joanna" (yes, now you're ready to be sick) as she must choose between the stuffy modern man who cannot express his feelings and the raw savage who understands her needs.

Good for losing weight, *The Piano* is fairly useless in every other category. It is a supercilious and fairly arrogant piece of work that subliminally tries to persuade us that we're stupid if we don't go with the nuances and allusions.

Take a tip from me: don't ever be bullied into liking rubbish because you think you have to. It's OK to find *The Piano* boring and ridiculous … because it is.

The Piano Teacher

A shy and repressed music teacher tries to veer away from intimacy and prefers self-harm until she is pursued by an obsessed pupil.

Director	Michael Haneke
Writer	Michael Haneke (from Elfriede Jelinek's book)
Starring	Isabelle Huppert
	Annie Girardot
	Benoît Magimel
Released	2001
Awards	Won 10 awards, including the Grand Prize of the Jury, Best Actress and Best Actor at Cannes, and nominated for the Golden Palm. Annie Girardot won Best Supporting Actress at the Césars, and Isabelle Huppert was nominated.
Box office	Worldwide US$ figure unavailable

"Haneke reveals that the emotionally arid discipline of Erika's musical life, and the sado-masochism of her relations with her students and her mother, have turned her into a world-class sociopath… *The Piano Teacher* is Euro art-shock porn. But that is to overlook its cold and steely brilliance: an inspired nightmare – chamber music for a chamber of horrors." Peter Bradshaw, *Guardian*

"The movie … turns Austria's passion for high culture into something akin to the dark monolith in *2001: A Space Odyssey*. It seems to drive people to grief, pain, torment and neurosis – or certainly, that potential lies dangerously close to the surface." Desson Howe, *Washington Post*

I've tried to leave French cinema alone. We already know that by and large a lot of it is nonsense, but thankfully the chattering classes seem to have forgotten it since the death of Truffaut (give or take the occasional odd film with Charlotte Rampling), so I thought it best to leave the Gallic movies well and truly undisturbed.

But if you're talking about overrated pictures you just cannot ignore *The Piano Teacher* (what is it about having the word piano in the title that makes movies so rubbish?). This is yet another "dark exposé of the uncharted world of sexual repression" that just passes me by.

The scene in particular where Isabelle Huppert's character apparently cuts her sexual bits and bobs is much lauded. Sorry – I have no interest whatsoever. There might be lots of young ladies sitting on scissors as we speak, but I don't care. And I certainly don't want to see it unless there's a proper point instead of wide-ranging generalizations about "psycho-sexual collapse".

The film goes from bad to worse as she starts to break away from her own sexual repression, with loud piano music in the background. Nothing here has anything relevant to say to me, or any intrigue. It appears to be shock for shock's sake. Stick a bit of classical music in there just so people know it's art and not exploitation (always helps if it's not in English too), and voilà – we are presented with a portrait of inner turmoil rather than a tacky sick DVD that should only be sold to people with "special interests" over the internet.

The Pink Panther

The biggest diamond in the world attracts leading gems thief, the mysterious Phantom, to a Swiss skiing resort, followed by a bumbling French police inspector.

Director	Blake Edwards
Writers	Blake Edwards, Maurice Richlin
Starring	David Niven
	Peter Sellers
	Robert Wagner
	Capucine
Released	1963
Awards	The score was nominated for an Oscar and a Grammy and won an ASCAP award for Most Performed Feature Film Standards in 1988. Peter Sellers was nominated for a BAFTA, a Golden Globe and a Golden Laurel. The screenplay won Best Written American Comedy at the Writers Guild of America.
Box office	Worldwide US$ figure unavailable
Tagline	A madcap frolic of crime and fun.

"In which Peter Sellers systematically, and decisively, destroys the world's perception of the French as sophisticated and cultured." Clayton Trapp, *Brilliant Observations on 1173 Films*

"If not for Sellers's hilarious pratfalls, *The Pink Panther* could be mistaken for a luxuriant caper movie like *Topkapi*, which is precisely what makes the movie so funny. It acts as the straight man, while Sellers gets to play mischief-maker." Scott Tobias, The Onion A.V. Club

This is more a little history lesson than anything else. Everyone thinks they love *The Pink Panther*. They will tell you that the sequels started to get annoying, but the original is so, so funny, etc. They're lying (or at least memory is playing tricks on them). What they're actually talking about is *A Shot in the Dark* (1964), an off-shoot rather than sequel, which for the first time concentrated on the Peter Sellers character.

The Pink Panther is actually a rather tedious David Niven-led drawing room farce that is only livened up in patches by the secondary character of Inspector Clouseau. It's a fairly mannered piece with people hiding in cupboards and under beds, uncle and nephew trying to steal the same jewel without the other knowing, and everyone dressing up for dinner.

It is not until Sellers takes over the scenes he is in (and allegedly they built more around him as the movie went on) that any laughs are garnered. *The Pink Panther* is a movie distinctly of its time that looks sadly faded and dated now (despite some nice touches by Niven who could do this role in his sleep). The pacing drags in many areas and the premise is too shallow to sustain a full feature. Without the emergence of Clouseau, the film, and the fantastic Mancini theme tune, would have sunk without a trace. We wouldn't even have had the obviously drug-inspired TV series. And that would have been a real disaster.

Platoon

A young soldier is faced with the inhumanity of man when he goes on a tour of duty in Vietnam.

Director	Oliver Stone
Writer	Oliver Stone
Starring	Tom Berenger
	Willem Dafoe
	Charlie Sheen
	Forest Whitaker
Released	1986
Awards	Won four Oscars for Best Picture, Director, Sound and Film Editing, and nominated for four more. Two BAFTAs for Editing and Direction, and nominated for Cinematography. Three Golden Globes, four Independent Spirit Awards, a Peace award from the Political Film Society, awards from the Casting Society and Directors Guild of America, and so on…
Box office	$152,963,328 (Worldwide)
Tagline	The first casualty of war is innocence.

"A film that says … that before you can make any vast, sweeping statements about Vietnam, you have to begin by understanding the bottom line, which is that a lot of people went over there and got killed, dead, and that is what the war meant for them." Roger Ebert, *Chicago Sun-Times*

"Oliver Stone's impression of the Vietnam War, taken from when he observed it first-hand as a grunt." Dennis Schwartz, Ozus' World Movie Reviews

"Stone was able to portray the war so accurately because he himself had a tour of duty in Vietnam." Marty Mapes, *Movie Habit*

"Like no other movie could tell, *Platoon* shows us categorically that war – and especially the Vietnam War – is hell." Christopher Null, FilmCritic.com

Yes Oliver, we know you were in Vietnam. We know you're owed some form of debt by the American government. But does that really mean that we have to suffer films like *Platoon*. I was only just born when you were over there shooting "gooks" or "geeks" or whatever they're called. It's not my fault, so don't take it out on me.

As themes go, "war is bad" is not a bad one. But there really does need to be more substance to make a movie. When you compare *Platoon* to masterpieces such as *Full Metal Jacket* (1987) and *The Deer Hunter* (1978), films that decided to have a structure and something definite to say, it's hard to work out why *Platoon* got so much praise. It must have been fear of contradicting Stone. He's a loud and imposing man at the best of times and, as we know, he was there. So no one was brave enough to actually say that the film isn't that good.

And sorry Oliver, it isn't. It may have Willem Dafoe in it (which always means that there's something interesting there), and we've picked up the hint that you were there, but *Platoon* doesn't actually blow you away (excuse the pun).

There's no real story, far too many indistinguishable characters that just merge into each other, and little in the way of action. It may show us what war is really like – but I didn't pay to go to war, I paid to see a movie.

Pollock

The story of expressionist painter Jackson Pollock – his breakthroughs, successes, and hidden demons.

Director	Ed Harris
Writers	Barbara Turner, Susan J. Emshwiller (from Steven Naifeh and Gregory White Smith's book)
Starring	Ed Harris
	Marcia Gay Harden
	Tom Bower
	Jennifer Connelly
Released	2000
Awards	Marcia Gay Harden won an Oscar and Ed Harris was nominated for Best Actor. The New York Film Critics Circle gave Marcia Gay Harden Best Supporting Actress, and Ed Harris got Best Actor from the Toronto Film Critics Association.
Box office	Worldwide US$ figure unavailable
Tagline	A true portrait of life and art.

"… a quietly excellent movie, clearly a labour of love for Harris, and far superior to much of the current Hollywood product. It is aimed at educated adults." Peter Bradshaw, *Guardian*

And what a load of old pollocks this was. A pretentious actor decides to make a movie about a pretentious painter ... I thought that two negatives were supposed to give us a positive. There's little positive here, although there's a fantastic, unintentionally laugh-out-loud moment, when the "artist" drips some paint on his canvas. He looks down and the light bulb of "eureka" comes on.

I feel really sorry for Marcia Gay Harden (a name that sounds vaguely rude), a brilliant actress who struggles on relentlessly with the role of his long-suffering wife who gives up her own career to care for him. But in an example of art almost following life, Ed Harris tries to over-act her out of every scene they share ("hey little lady, this is my tortured film"). In a piece of ironic justice she did actually win an Oscar for her troubles, but why were the old buffers at the Academy watching this pile of drivel in the first place?

Like Pollock's work, this film is a messy and lazy muddle that "experts" have taken far too seriously. The whole inner-demons-of-the-artist concept is clichéd and mundane, especially when the subject is only splattering a wee bit of paint onto a canvas. We never actually get to see what his problem is, and how we might be able to solve it. But as it's Ed Harris (a wannabe Malkovich who just doesn't come close), making a film about an artist, people were afraid to condemn.

The Producers

A pair of chancers come up with the ultimate scam: raise more money than you need for a guaranteed Broadway flop, the investors will not be expecting a return and you can keep the surplus.

Director	Mel Brooks
Writer	Mel Brooks
Starring	Zero Mostel
	Gene Wilder
Released	1968
Awards	Best Screenplay at the Oscars, and Gene Wilder was nominated for Best Supporting Actor. Mel Brooks also won an award for the screenplay from the Writers Guild of America and was nominated for another. Nominated for two Golden Globes, for the screenplay and for Zero Mostel.
Box office	Worldwide US$ figure unavailable
Tagline	Hollywood never faced a zanier zero hour.

"This shamelessly low-brow, fearlessly satirical Brooks movie may just be Hollywood's ultimate satire, a furiously witty 'reductio ad absurdum' worthy of the great Augustans like Pope and Swift." Susan Stark, *Detroit News*, Rotten Tomatoes

Forget the recent musical – it wasn't any good, and people said it wasn't any good. But the original holds a real affection in movie history. Which is a shame because it's also not very good.

The Producers has a nice premise, but little else. Most of the film consists of Zero Mostel and Gene Wilder shouting at each other. The idea of *Springtime for Hitler*, the musical, is edgy and funny. But it's also slightly disingenuous. Only a Jewish director could have gotten away with it. If *The Producers* had been the brainchild of a Gentile he would have been run out of Hollywood (even more so in these PC days).

And it's a real shame if the man who made *Young Frankenstein* (1974) and *Blazing Saddles* (1974) is to be remembered for this piece of fluff (*Spaceballs* (1987) is better). It is a one-joke movie that starts to grate very early, and long outstays its welcome.

Apart from our shouting double-act we are fed with an array of over the top and uninteresting comic characters like the gay director and Nazi writer, who constantly fail to tickle the funny bones.

The Producers could have been a nice and edgy *Saturday Night Live* sketch, but it has been stretched and overblown into a tiresome and cumbersome one-joke-movie. It's not inspired lunacy, as it's been labelled by so many (look at *Hellzapoppin* (1941) for that), or even hysterically funny (although some form of mass hysteria must have gone into creating its popularity). It's loud, boorish and unfunny.

Proof

The daughter of a recently deceased mathematician claims that she solved a crucial theory that was attributed to her father, making people suspect that she has merely inherited his insanity.

Director	John Madden
Writers	David Auburn, Rebecca Miller
Starring	Gwyneth Paltrow
	Anthony Hopkins
	Jake Gyllenhaal
Released	2005
Awards	Stephen Warbeck, the composer, won the Georges Delerue Prize at the Flanders International Film Festival, and John Madden was nominated for a Golden Spur there, and a Golden Lion at the Venice Film Festival. Gwyneth Paltrow was nominated for a Golden Globe.
Box office	Worldwide US$ figure unavailable
Tagline	The biggest risk in life is not taking one.

"… John Madden has woven together an elegant, intelligent drama of a breed increasingly rare in mainstream American movies." David Rooney, *Variety*

"Gwyneth Paltrow reveals new depths and never plays for easy sympathy." Philip French, *Observer*

Oh great – a film that has Gwynnie in it for nearly 80% of the screen time, what could be better? Oh look, we've got hammie Anthony Hopkins there just for good measure. Any film that gets these two terrible actors together is obviously going to be terrible. Paltrow has little range ("chewing on a lemon peel" being her most usual facial expression) and no charisma. Hopkins got lucky once, thanks to Jodie Foster carrying him, and has fooled people ever since (more is not less Tony, so stop overacting).

Add to that a rather woeful and stagey script that couldn't actually decide what it's about and you end up with the self-opinionated and dreary mess that is *Proof*. Mathematics is never a zinger of a movie topic anyway (see *A Beautiful Mind*), and layering on gooey stratum of navel-gazing will not help that particular conundrum.

If our expressionless lead actress had given us something to recognize and go along with then we might have forgiven many of *Proof*'s failings. But as it is we don't care whether she wrote this mysterious mathematical puzzle or not. We don't care if she's going crazy. All we care about is when we're going to escape the cinema and this inconsequential dross.

Good old Jake Gyllenhaal tries to inject a little bit of humanity and interest into the proceedings, but hampered by the pompous and self-important script he finally gives up – and so did I.

Bad performances, ambivalent premise, woeful dialogue, no sense of pacing … you do the maths.

Raising Arizona

A childless couple decide to steal a baby from a family
who have quins. Well, they're not going to miss one, are
they?

Directors	Joel Cohen, Ethan Cohen
Writers	Joel Cohen, Ethan Cohen
Starring	Nicolas Cage
	Holly Hunter
	Trey Wilson
	John Goodman
Released	1987
Awards	Nominated for Best Family Motion Picture – Comedy at the Young Artist Awards
Box office	Worldwide US$ figure unavailable
Tagline	A comedy beyond belief.

"*Raising Arizona* possesses such a bounty of thematic offerings
that, despite its objective strengths, no praise matches the
height of my own commendation." Rumsey Taylor, Not Coming
to a Theater Near You, Rotten Tomatoes.com

The Cohen brothers are cinematic masters, of that there is no question. They have provided me personally with some of my happiest movie experiences – from *Barton Fink* (1991) to *Oh Brother Where Art Thou?* (2000), and not (indeed never) forgetting *Fargo* (1996) and the sublime *The Big Lebowski* (1998). But it's got to be said that they did drop the ball somewhat on *Raising Arizona*.

After the stunningly original and lively *Blood Simple* (1984) the critics were expecting rolled gold again with *Raising Arizona*, and they weren't prepared to say otherwise just because the film isn't very good.

The movie mostly falls down due to over-the-top performances from Nic Cage and Holly Hunter, an extremely empty premise (stupid couple try to hide a baby), and the slavish reliance on the audience going goo-goo at the cute infant.

You can't be too hard on the film as the brothers obviously learned their lessons. But it is painful to hear people still raving about *Raising Arizona* like they had seen some kind of messianic vision.

Don't be convinced by their cult-like rants. Watching this film is an empty experience, and you can only be saddened by the clichéd chase scenes and fist fights. With the pressure after *Blood Simple*, the brothers were obviously trying much too hard, and the whole movie screams "look at me, look at me, aren't I wacky and zany?" And the truth is, it's not.

The best way to sum it up is to take *Every Which Way But Loose* (1978), substitute the orang-utan for a baby, and you've got *Raising Arizona*.

Ray

The life of legendary blues man Ray Charles

Director	Taylor Hackford
Writers	Taylor Hackford, James L. White
Starring	Jamie Foxx
	Kerry Washington
	Regina King
Released	2004
Awards	This film won 39 awards and got 36 nominations. Jamie Foxx won an Oscar, and the film won the Best Achievement in Sound award. Jamie also won a BAFTA, A Black Reel award, a Golden Globe, an Image award and a Satellite award. There were various awards for the soundtrack, including two Grammys, and assorted awards for other actors and aspects of the movie.
Box office	$111,805,995 (Worldwide)
Tagline	The extraordinary life story of Ray Charles. A man who fought harder and went farther than anyone thought possible.

"*Ray* is, quite simply, one of the most outstanding biographical movies that I have ever seen and, by far, one of the better movies that I have seen this year." Erin Cullin, *Empire Movies*

Another long and tedious movie from the man who gave us *An Officer and a Gentleman* (1982) – Taylor Hackford. Famous for being married to Helen Mirren and ... well, apart from Richard Gere carrying the woman out of the factory, very little.

And here, yet again, the laws of biopic are completely forgotten. There has to be a point Taylor! You can't just do a film where the protagonist does this ... and then this ... and then this ... ad nauseam. Films need a theme and a direction, and *Ray* has neither.

Yes, the music is great. It really makes you want to go out and buy some Ray Charles CDs. But the rest of the entertainment is minimal and we would have been much better off seeing the real man in concert.

Jamie Foxx is an accomplished actor. But here, rather like Robert Downey Junior in *Chaplin* (1992), he does an impression rather than giving a performance. It is a very good impression, granted; but I'm sure there are better Ray Charles tribute acts out there that we could watch if we really want to (and his distinctive head wobbling and grin probably make it easier than it seems to take him off).

But I wanted to learn about the real man – how his blindness drove him on, his drug-taking, his adultery and the reaction from his wife, the racist problems he encountered. But none of these are properly investigated here. Unlike Mr. Spock's ear, *Ray* does not have a point. There's no proper narrative structure and everything is super superficial. This makes his life, and the film, feel awfully long and boring. Which is a huge sin when you've got such an interesting core subject.

Ray isn't the only one who was blind in this project.

Rebel Without a Cause

A young rebel comes to a new town and creates havoc, causing distress and anger to his middle class parents, the police, his neighbours and even his new friends.

Director	Nicholas Ray
Writers	Nicholas Ray, Irving Shulman, Stewart Stern
Starring	James Dean
	Natalie Wood
	Sal Mineo
Released	1955
Awards	Sal Mineo, Natalie Wood and Nicholas Ray for the story were all nominated for Oscars, James Dean was nominated for a BAFTA as was the film as Best Film from any Source.
Box office	Worldwide US$ figure unavailable
Tagline	Jim Stark … a kid from a "good" family – what makes him tick … like a bomb?

"Profoundly romantic and lacerating in its despair…" Dan Callahan, *Slant* magazine

"*Rebel* really belongs entirely to Dean and his iconic red windbreaker. Everyone else revolves around him and fades in the bright light of his on-screen charisma." Don Willmott, FilmCritic.com

Teen angst my ass. This is a tame (even for the time) load of nonsense which tried to make Dean look cool and dangerous, without being too threatening. If it talks to you that means you must be an affected middle-class teenager with damn all to do but complain.

The movie's a fake – it's phoney from start to finish. There's nothing edgy or dangerous about it, and who the hell cares about prissy too-rich teenagers? Give 'em a smack. Honestly, I just found Dean's character a right pain. Problems? He had no problems, except for too much time on his hands and a useless set of parents. And, of course, it all works out in the end.

Dean became a style icon simply for driving too fast and being a bit of a twat (Michael Schumacher's been trying to achieve the same ever since).

Dean wasn't really the star of *Rebel Without a Cause*, the red jacket was. Without the distinctive jacket he wouldn't have looked half as good and would never have appeared on numerous students' walls and girls' pencil cases. They've never seen the film – lots of people haven't bothered seeing the film. They don't have to. They know it stars someone who is famous for dying before giving a good performance, and that red jacket. And they know the famous quote "What are you rebelling against? What have you got?" (ridiculous line that it is).

So don't feel bad if you haven't sat through *Rebel Without a Cause* – you've had a lucky escape. Don't feel you need to now, and definitely don't feel that you're missing something. Take five minutes in a clothes shop, stare at a red jacket, and that's all you need.

A Room with a View

After her visit to Florence, and her encounter with George, England (and her fiancé) just don't look the same to Lucy.

Director	James Ivory
Writer	Ruth Prawer Jhabvala (from E. M. Forster's book)
Starring	Maggie Smith
	Helena Bonham-Carter
	Denholm Elliott
	Julian Sands
	Simon Callow
Released	1985
Awards	Won three Oscars for Costumes, Screenplay and Art Direction, and nominated for five more. Five BAFTAs and nominated for nine more. James Ivory got an award from the Directors Guild of America, Ruth Prawer Jhabvala got one from the Writers Guild of America, Maggie Smith won a Golden Globe, and so on…
Box office	Worldwide US$ figure unavailable

"This is the best film [Merchant-Ivory] have made. It is an intellectual film… *A Room with a View* enjoys its storytelling so much that I enjoyed the very process of it. The story moved slowly, it seemed, for the same reason you try to make ice cream last: because it's so good." Roger Ebert, *Chicago Sun-Times*

Think of this as a time-saving measure. For this entry consider every damned dull and tiresome Merchant-Ivory production. This is possibly the worst, and the one that was best received, although the sheep tended to coo (oh dear, bad mixed metaphor there) over most of them. Merchant and Ivory have made a career of taking bad and overrated novels and making them into stiff and lifeless films (that were well received from people that can't differentiate culture from agriculture).

In this particularly drab and empty epic they fool the audience into thinking they should be understanding the unstated sensuality. Don't be fooled. You won't recognize the subtext because there's none there. Merchant-Ivory films' greatest success is fooling a stupid audience into thinking there's more here than meets the eye. In fact, there's less.

The movies are flat, undemanding and incredibly bland. Merchant-Ivory take staid and unremarkable novels from very average writers (E. M. Forster, Henry James, Jane Austen). They then put a "sheen of class" over it by casting acclaimed British actors and shooting with a tub of Vaseline over the lens.

The underdeveloped minds of the chattering classes then are fooled into believing that there's some greater depth there that they can't see – but of course they won't admit to this. And so, hey presto: acclaimed cultural classics! Easy, isn't it?

Look at the career of Helena Bonham-Carter. She appeared a distinctly below-par actress in the Merchant-Ivory films; obviously told to look pretty and talk posh. Once she gets out of their clutches we get to see what an accomplished performer she really is.

You don't have to be able to act to be in a Merchant-Ivory film (in fact, it doesn't even help). Like the films, all you have to do is appear classy.

Run Lola Run

Three different stories with the same starting point: a young woman has 20 minutes to get a sizeable amount of cash to her boyfriend and thus save his life.

Director	Tom Tykwer
Writer	Tom Tykwer
Starring	Franka Potente
	Moritz Bleibtreu
Released	1998
Awards	This film won 29 awards including seven at the German Film Awards, the World Cinema audience award at Sundance, and the Golden Space Needle award at the Seattle International Film Festival. It was nominated for a BAFTA for Best Film not in the English Language amongst its 12 nominations.
Box office	Worldwide US$ figure unavailable
Tagline	Every second of every day you're faced with a decision that can change your life.

"… a sort of power-pop variation on the mystical time-bending Euro-art movies made by the late Krzysztof Kieslowski."
J. Hoberman, *Village Voice*

"When you can sum up a story in one sentence you know you have a great one. 'Lola has twenty minutes to come up with 100,000 marks and run through the city to rescue her true love.' And she does it, and then she does it again, and then she does it again. Lola is amazing." DAK, culturevulture.net

Dear, dear me. How did this foolish and simplistic film ever get out of the starting blocks? It's not just a bad film, it's three bad films! A fairly unattractive German woman (don't look at the armpits) runs around and around, and around and around. All to save her prattish, unattractive boyfriend who we don't see enough of to care about.

The biggest flaw in *Run Lola Run* is that we're made aware after the first segment that this is a film; it's not real life. And with that suspension of disbelief gone there is no tension or energy to the piece. We never really cared for her boyfriend anyway, but now we don't even care about her and the race against time because we know she'll get another chance.

Without this all we're left with is a rather poor student film … and in German to boot (harsh and guttural). The camerawork is OK in places, although the look of the film is undoubtedly cold and flat. But without any emotional investment the idea of the audience being in the middle of the movie is a false hope. So while the pace keeps up it doesn't really matter as all the rest is inconsequential.

But those who think they know better than us mere mortals decided to discover the film, and the director. Suddenly he is the new Julian Schnabel (which, in a way, he is – overrated, untalented and foreign).

Saturday Night Fever

A young New Yorker doesn't care about anything else except for becoming the disco dancing champion, but eventually he has to face up to reality.

Director	John Badham
Writer	Norman Wexler (from Nik Cohn's magazine article)
Starring	John Travolta
	Karen Lynn Gorney
Released	1977
Awards	John Travolta won Best Actor from the Natrional Board of Review in the USA, and the film won a Golden Screen in Germany. John Travolta was also nominated for an Oscar, and the film got two BAFTA nominations and four Golden Globe nominations.
Box office	$285,400,000 (Worldwide)
Tagline	Where do you go when the record is over…

"One minute into *Saturday Night Fever* you know this picture is on to something, that it knows what it's talking about." Gene Siskel, *Chicago Tribune*, metacritic.com

Forget the nostalgia. Turn away from the excellent soundtrack, the costumes and the haircuts. Just watch *Saturday Night Fever* as a film for once. This was supposed to be a great film – in total contrast to *Grease* (1978), which came out around the same time, this was a real movie with a social conscience.

If you still believe that your head is tighter than the Bee Gees' trousers. *Saturday Night Fever* is a terrible movie that would have been laughed off screen if it hadn't have been for the music and the timing. If you don't believe me, watch it now – you'll be amazed at how you were fooled.

The story is simplistic, predictable and childish (almost junior school level). The dialogue is so bad that it positively creaks. The actors almost look apologetic and guilty when spitting out the ludicrous lines. The language refuses to take up a rhythm or communicate motivation, back story or action. Everything is obvious and long-winded.

But it probably always would be coming from Travolta. It's hard to imagine just how far John Travolta has come as an actual actor since *SNF*. His performance is so wooden that they should have got Pinocchio to play the role. His neck seems to be definitely made of wood – he takes forever to turn his head, pout and then utter the drivel that aspires to be dialogue.

What's most surprising is that the dancing isn't even that good. Most of the routines are staid, unimaginative and repetitive. You'd see better boogying on a Saturday night down the pub.

It is strange to note that *Grease* has stood the test of time much better. *Saturday Night Fever*, for all its grown-up 18 certificate and supposed social issues, is the film that more resembles the amateurish school show.

Scent of a Woman

A poor student agrees to look after a blind ex-army officer over Thanksgiving, but bites off more than he can chew when the old military man decides on a night to remember.

Director	Martin Brest
Writers	Bo Goldman, Ruggero Maccari, Dino Risi (from Giovanni Arpino's book)
Starring	Al Pacino Chris O'Donnell
Released	1992
Awards	Al Pacino won an Oscar, and the film got three more nominations. Three Golden Globes, including one for Al Pacino. Won a BMI Film music award. One BAFTA nomination for the screenplay.
Box office	Worldwide US$ figure unavailable
Tagline	Col. Frank Slade has a very special plan for the weekend. It involves travel, women, good food, fine wine, the tango, chauffeured limousines and a loaded forty-five. And he's taking Charlie along for the ride.

"Pacino's voice has always been a marvel, but it's been a long time since he's had a character that allowed him to showcase the full range of his talents." Hal Hinson, *Washington Post*

"His tango with a stranger (sexy Gabrielle Anwar) is courtly and poignant. Even with his expressive eyes locked in a fixed stare, Pacino hauntingly captures Slade's longing; he's astoundingly good." (uncredited) *Rolling Stone*

Once upon a time Al Pacino was seen as a very talented actor – one to look out for – and then he began shouting. And he has mistaken shouting for showing emotion ever since. When his character is happy, he shouts. When he's angry, he shouts. God help us if he ever has to simulate sex.

And Pacino has never been louder than in *Scent of a Woman*. He obviously misunderstood. Blind people usually have increased sense of hearing, not an increased tonsil capacity Al. Every scene goes up in decibels from the last, making the whole film a gruelling and harsh experience.

But even with all the shouting (or perhaps because of it) we're still really uncertain what this bloody awful picture is about – something to do with a man at the start of his life, and another one at the end. There's also stuff chucked in about both being let down by their friends. But it's all a loud, very loud mess that doesn't actually do anything.

Chris O'Donnell thankfully talks at a moderate tone until the plot goes haywire (and by then we've switched off all our senses anyway), but you've got to feel sorry for him. Pacino blares and overacts the whole time, leaving little Chris in a private movie of his own. Still, at least at this stage he had his whole career in front of him. That is, until *Batman Forever* (1995) and *In Love and War* (1996) killed him stone dead.

Maybe you should have shouted more Chris?

Sexy Beast

Gal is happily retired from his life of crime and living it up in Spain, but then an old boss shows up and insists that he comes back for one last job.

Director	Jonathan Glazer
Writers	Louis Mellis, David Scinto
Starring	Ray Winstone
	Ben Kingsley
	Ian McShane
	Amanda Redman
Released	2000
Awards	Won four British Independent Film Awards, including one for Ben Kingsley and one for Ray Winstone. Ben also won a European Film Award, a Satellite and awards from the San Diego, Southeastern and Toronto Film Critics Associations. He was nominated for a Golden Globe and an Oscar.
Box office	Worldwide US$ figure unavailable
Tagline	Sometimes it's hard to say no.

"An implacable amalgam of menace, vulgarity, bullheadedness and lunacy… This is Kingsley's best performance in years, maybe his best ever." Glenn Kenny, *Premiere*

Definitely the most overrated British film of the last decade, *Sexy Beast* is one that you definitely should give a swerve to (as us cock-a-knees would say). Which is a shame as the first scene is highly original, entertaining, intelligent and stays with you for a long, long time.

But like the boulder that rains down on Ray Winstone, it's all downhill from there. Most of this disappointment must go down to the incredibly annoying Ben (please call me Sir) Kingsley. His character, Don, has somehow become a modern icon. The Lord works in mysterious ways.

Rarely has there been a more preposterous and over-egged performance than this. You can't take him seriously as Don bears no resemblance to anyone living or dead. Thus we can't find him intimidating or threatening. He's not a gangster boss – it's a skinny thespian hamming it up in best RADA tradition dahling. And so in the end we are watching an all-star bout between Ray ("who's the daddy?") Winstone and Gandhi. Not even an Irish bookie would give you odds on that.

It's all such a shame. The idea, although derivative, is intriguing and engaging. The film does boast great performances from the reliable Winstone and Amanda Redman. Visually it looks great. But as soon as the little baldy fella hovers into shot the whole film falls to pieces. The story becomes less and less plausible and even the editing starts to look ropey and misguided. Maybe they were all laughing too much at Bendi's posturing, and couldn't concentrate on what they were doing?

Take that knighthood off him immediately (he's only really been good in one film, and even then all he had to do was smile quietly and spin himself another nappy) and give it to someone who deserves it much more. Arise Sir Winstone!

She's Gotta Have It

A young black woman in New York is happy with her three lovers, but they all want to have her to themselves.

Director	Spike Lee
Writer	Spike Lee
Starring	Tracy Camilla Johns
	Tommy Redmond Hicks
	John Canada Terrell
	Spike Lee
Released	1986
Awards	Won an Award of the Youth at Cannes and a New Generation Award from the Los Angeles Film Critics Association. It won Best First Feature at the Independent Spirit awards, and Tracy Camilla Johns was nominated for Best Female Lead
Box office	Worldwide US$ figure unavailable
Tagline	A seriously sexy comedy.

"A good first effort that lacks quality acting and overall polish, but compensates with insightful black man's humor." Dennis Schwartz, Ozus' World Movie Reviews

She's Gotta Have It sums up all the hypocrisy of 1980s political correctness. If this film had been about a man with three woman lovers, who all wanted to "own" him it would have been chased out of every college town in the western world. But same story, different sex, and suddenly we are supposed to applaud the director's vision and originality. It also helps that the director and cast are all black, giving the white middle-class "opinion makers" a cause célèbre that will enhance their pc credentials.

Get off your high horses people! You obviously can't see the screen properly from your ivory towers (oh dear, yet another mixed metaphor). *She's Gotta Have It* was a fairly tawdry, very pleased with itself, extremely boring film that should never have seen the light of day. As a comedy it isn't funny (although Lee obviously thinks his own small role in the film is hilarious), and it is much less sexy than it thinks it is. The film is also not liberated or feminist, as many of its blind followers claim. In fact *She's Gotta Have It* does real harm to every feminist ideal.

A little like Ian McKellen shoving his sexuality down peoples' throats (ooh er), Spike Lee is far too keen to be black to concentrate on making good movies. Mr. Lee, we know you're black. Most of us don't care. We'd rather be entertained than preached at. The only ones really taking your message are the middle-class whites. The Wayans boys have actually done much better work as spokespeople and inspiration for the American blacks than Spike Lee has ever done. And *White Chicks* (2004) kicks *She's Gotta Have It*s ass all over the pitch.

Shine

A talented young pianist is pushed too hard by his family and teachers and suffers a breakdown, but years later he rediscovers himself through the piano.

Director	Scott Hicks
Writers	Scott Hicks, Jan Sardi
Starring	Geoffrey Rush
	Justin Braine
	Sonia Todd
Released	1996
Awards	39 awards and 33 nominations. Geoffrey Rush got a Golden Globe, a Screen Actors Guild award and an Oscar, and the film received six more Oscar nominations. It won nine Australian Film Institute awards and got three more nominations, and two BAFTAs with seven more nominations. You get the idea.
Box office	$89,111,509 (Worldwide)
Tagline	A true story of the mystery of music and the miracle of love.

"Audaciously directed by Scott Hicks from an unconventional script by Jan Sardi, *Shine* is also utterly extraordinary: biography without banality, uplift without upchuck, art without artifice. Rank it with the very best movies of the year." (uncredited) *Rolling Stone*

Sorry, have I missed something here? A man on a trampoline … interesting enough, although I prefer the footage of Claudia Schiffer on a trampoline in the Nic Roeg short. But that's really about it, isn't it? What else is there in *Shine* to keep us amused? We have a Jewish boy (lots of clichés here) who has a nervous breakdown because he can't play a tune on the piano (maybe he should learn to relax and not take things too seriously?). We then flash forward to a bit of a nutter, who plays the piano again. Not much of a film is it?

I went into *Shine* not being much of an expert on Rachmaninoff's *Piano Concerto Number Three*, and I'm still not (except I now know that it's slightly harder to play than "Chopsticks"). I knew even less about being a young Jewish boy in Australia, and I still don't. And I went into *Shine* not knowing the point of the movie, and I still don't.

What's it all about? Why are we watching it? With this film it's not just that I can't understand why people extol its virtues so, I can't even work out what the virtues are supposed to be.

I really did find *Shine* a very empty and purposeless movie. It is episodic and jumpy, with little to appreciate or empathize with. The usually reliable Armin Mueller-Stahl is fairly clichéd and poor old Lynn Redgrave should never have even thought of taking her part. Geoffrey Rush is OK, although it's kinda easy to play such an overblown personality – much harder to be a real person. But let's be honest … he's no Claudia Schiffer.

Sideways

For a bachelor weekend two middle-aged men tour the wineries of California; both of them are seeking different things from the trip and neither of them have found happiness from their lives.

Director	Alexander Payne
Writers	Alexander Payne, Jim Taylor (from Rex Pickett's book)
Starring	Paul Giamatti
	Thomas Haden Church
	Virginia Madsen
	Sandra Oh
Released	2004
Awards	92 awards and 31 nominations. Won an Oscar for the screenplay, and received four more nominations. One BAFTA for the screeplay, two Golden Globes and five nominations, six Independent Spirit awards, the Cast award from the Screen Actors Guild, loads of Film Critics Circle awards...
Box office	$85,902,303 (Worldwide)
Tagline	In search of wine. In search of women. In search of themselves.

"New classics of American cinema don't come along that often, so grab this one with both hands... *Sideways* is beautifully written, terrifically acted; it is paced and constructed with such understated mastery that it is a sort of miracle." Peter Bradshaw, *Guardian*

My oh my, did the film community get conned by this one. A slow, pretentious and fairly drab movie is suddenly acclaimed by one and all as a masterpiece. This could have been because they recognized some of the characters' disappointment in their own empty lives, or they might just have been pissed before they went in, but whatever it is *Sideways* really did make the emperor seem underdressed.

It is unlikely that ever before so much has been spouted about so little. The film is neither funny nor uplifting, and the underlying themes are ambivalent and ill-defined. Possibly funded by the Californian tourist board and the local wine industry (it appears that every newspaper travel section has to have a *Sideways* piece at least once a year by law now), the movie manages to be pretentious while supposedly stripping away the pretentiousness of the main character.

Its main flaw is how slow the film is; you really do feel you've been with them for the whole weekend. A gentle pace is fine, especially for a grown-up movie, but this is almost static. Also, it's supposed to be a comedy. When you find the film desperately trying to eke out laughs from a man drinking a spit bucket you know you're in serious trouble.

And the premise was just too ridiculous. These two men could not be lifelong friends; they're not Felix and Oscar, they're two extremely separate people from separate lives who just would not become close acquaintances. Plus the bridegroom-to-be wanted a weekend of debauchery, so he would not have agreed to go on a genteel trip around vineyards. And so you fail to go with the movie right from the start, making the rest of the action (for what action there is) completely immaterial.

The fact that *Sideways* became so popular is ironically a little like the snobbery you encounter in the enjoyment of wine. No one was willing to be the first to say that this film is corked.

Sliding Doors

Just how would your life change because of the split second difference between getting the train or having to wait for the next?

Director	Peter Howitt
Writer	Peter Howitt
Starring	Gwyneth Paltrow
	John Hannah
	John Lynch
	Jeanne Tripplehorn
Released	1998
Awards	Won a BAFTA for Best British Film, an Empire Award for Best British Director, a European Film Award and a San Diego Film Critics Society award for the screenplay. Gwyneth Paltrow received a Special Award in San Diego as well as Best Foreign Actress from the Russian Guild of Film Critics. The film was nominated for a Golden Seashell at the San Sebastián International Film Festival.
Box office	$67,183,495 (Worldwide)
Tagline	What if one split second sent your life in two completely different directions?

"*Sliding Doors* was a success largely deserved as director/ screenwriter Peter Howitt finds an original way to breathe new life into the Brit take on romantic comedy." Ian Freer, Britmovie. co.uk

Please do not misunderstand. This book is not a personal diatribe against Gwyneth Paltrow. But it is no coincidence that the very overrated actress is listed in so many of these films. Let's be honest, anyone who saw her speech at the Oscars some years ago will agree that she even has real difficulty being convincing in the role of Ms. G. Paltrow.

Here her questionable talents are pitted alongside John Lynch, a particularly flat and expressionless actor; and the very overrated John Hannah. This film was damned from the start.

But *Sliding Doors* was never acclaimed because of the performances. Even the most shallow of critics could see that this was not going to be an impromptu acting class from three masters of the profession. No, *Sliding Doors* was heralded to the rooftops because of the "ingenious" premise. What utter rot.

It is ingenious to show a man what the world would be like if he had never lived by introducing him to his guardian angel. It's nothing short of plain silly to wonder what would happen if we didn't make the tube and then split the story in two (both, confusingly, happening at the same time). To differentiate between the on-train Gwynie and the on-platform Gwynie we were also fed the "ingenious" device of one of them getting her hair cut (couldn't they just have blacked her up?).

Don't listen to what they say. *Sliding Doors* has no inherent charm or romance. It is not funny (always a drawback in a comedy, I find) and the leading man, who we should be rooting for, is an annoying prat who quotes Monty Python and apparently goes rowing down the Thames (don't we all?).

I really wish I'd stayed on the platform and not bothered going to see it in the first place.

Something Wild

A staid businessman thinks he is getting a lift to the office, but instead he is kidnapped by an outlandish woman who wants him to play the part of her husband at her high school reunion. But her real husband has just got out of prison and is not happy.

Director	Jonathan Demme
Writer	E. Max Frye
Starring	Jeff Daniels
	Melanie Griffith
Released	1986
Awards	Ray Liotta won an award from the Boston Society of Filmm Critics, and E. Max Frye won an Edgar Allen Poe award. The film was nominated for Best Casting by the Casting Society of America, and nominated for three Golden Globes for Jeff Daniels, Melanie Griffiths and Ray Liotta.
Box office	Worldwide US$ unavailable
Tagline	Something different something daring something dangerous

"This is one of those rare movies where the plot seems surprised at what the characters do." Roger Ebert, *Chicago Sun-Times*

"There may be no greater test of a filmmaker's talent than whether he can inject his own personality into a routine commercial script, and in that regard, Jonathan Demme's *Something Wild* is a triumph. It's also a load of fun." Paul Attanasio, *Washington Post*

A new genre began in the 1980s – the yuppie nightmare. This has been expanded and developed since, but the basic premise was that an ambitious and hard working person is suddenly thrown off-kilter. *Something Wild* was heralded as the epitome of yuppie nightmare films … for no apparent reason.

Put this mishmash of stupidity and predictability against strong yuppie nightmare comedies such as Scorsese's *After Hours* (1985), or even the little seen *The Michelle Apts* (1995) and you can see how Demme's film positively shrinks in comparison.

The main problem is, of course, Melanie Griffith. As an actress she can be fairly annoying, but in *Something Wild* she hits depths she only ever managed to equal as Kit Devereux in the must-see-because-it's-so-dreadful *Shadow of Doubt* (1998). Her character here, "Lulu" (yeah, right), is supposed to be a wild free spirit – someone who rails against authority and is totally "out there". But she's never convincing. She is also supposed to be incredibly sexy. Nope, sorry she hit a bum note with that too (with or without the stupid black wig).

And so despite the best efforts of Jeff Daniels (in his usual role, but one that he always does effectively), and Ray Liotta (a man whose career never took off as well as it should have), plus a decent soundtrack (Demme isn't a great film maker, but he's always got a good choice in music) the whole film collapses around them.

It's not wild, or fun, or rebellious, or even faintly diverting.

Sylvia

The life of poet Sylvia Plath whose insecurities, and her husband's infidelities, lead her to commit suicide.

Director	Christine Jeffs
Writer	John Brownlow
Starring	Gwyneth Paltrow
	Daniel Craig
	Jared Harris
	Blythe Danner
	Michael Gambon
Released	2003
Awards	Won an award of distinction from the Australian Cinematographers Society
Box office	Worldwide US$ figure unavailable
Tagline	Life was too small to contain her…

"Given the awe-inspiring odds against, Christine Jeffs's *Sylvia* is one of the most heroic literary biopics of recent years. It's short on complexity, poetry and detail. Purists will fume like Victorian chimney stacks. But the raw power of the performances by Gwyneth Paltrow and Daniel Craig touch nerves that run far deeper than John Brownlow's pot-boiling script. It's a chemical masterpiece." James Christopher, *The Times*

Never before have I been so keen for a person to hurry up and commit suicide! I'm surprised that most of the audience didn't follow her inspiration after having to sit through such an appalling waste of good celluloid.

Why would the makers ever think that we might be interested in the insecurities of Sylvia Plath (even if she was married to James Bond)? It's a dull life and a depressing finish. Were those literally tens of Sylvia Plath fans really screaming to see a portrayal of their heroine? I think not. Writing poetry is not the most visually exciting of pastimes anyway, but *Sylvia* goes one better by showing someone not writing poetry. It must make the UK taxpayers feel proud that their hard-earned money went to make such an obviously commercial picture.

The main problem is that people who went to Cambridge have some strange sense that everyone else would like to know about the university. Then the mealy-mouthed, polytechnic-educated critics get to see the results. Shamed by their own apparent lack of grounding in the arts they're happy to pretend that they understand and appreciate these smug cinematic efforts.

And *Sylvia* is the perfect example – tortured artist, 1950s Cambridge, lots of poetry: what more could the unwashed plebs want? Well, it would be nice to have a character that is accessible, convincing and interesting. A decent storyline, faster pacing and a structure that is not so horrendously linear would also be help. If only they taught film-making at Cambridge.

And see? I didn't mention Gwynie once!

The Talented Mr. Ripley

A Machiavellian young American ingratiates himself into the life of a spoilt rich playboy, but then he is unceremoniously dropped from the social scene.

Director	Anthony Minghella
Writer	Anthony Minghella (from Patricia Highsmith's book)
Starring	Matt Damon
	Gwyneth Paltrow
	Jude Law
	Cate Blanchett
	Philip Seymour Hoffman
	Jack Davenport
Released	1999
Awards	Eight wins, but 51 nominations. Jude Law won a BAFTA, and the film got six more nominations. He also got a Blockbuster Entertainment Award, with three more nominations. Other notable nominations were for five Oscars and five Golden Globes.
Box office	$125,292,135 (Worldwide)
Tagline	How far would you go to become someone else.

"… the best Alfred Hitchcock movie made since Alfred Hitchcock died." Tom Block, Culture Vulture

"… this is an instant classic, not in the sense that the word is typically applied to movies – as a synonym for masterpiece, though it is that too – but how we use the word to describe cars and clothes, embodying clean lines, subtle elegance, and a sense of timelessness." MaryAnn Johanson, Flick Filosopher

This is a pompous and showy film that absolutely demands that you pay it respect. The overwhelming tone is of self-satisfied arrogance. It almost screams to you "if you don't like us you must be stupid."

Well don't be bullied. *The Talented Mr. Ripley* is a horrible exercise of style over content. It's not mischievous or intelligent. The film is in reality a poor literary adaptation which presumes too much and fails to deliver real suspense or intrigue.

It doesn't help that the Machiavellian murderer is played by a little boy (Damon) who would be more convincing serving as an altar-boy. Watch the delightful John Malkovich take the character to his heart in *Ripley's Game* (2002) and you realize exactly what *The Talented Mr. Ripley* is missing. We want a character that we love to hate, hate to love, but still enjoy marvelling at his amoral attitude to this world. Ripley is the person we all want to be if we only had the nerve, looks, sophistication and intelligence. Matt Damon probably doesn't even want to be Matt Damon. Our Ripley here is bland and dull, with little sense of fun or edge.

Jude Law is as camp and insignificant as ever in this very ordinary film. We don't know whether we're supposed to hate his character, and cheer our antihero on, or sympathize with him. This ambivalence really kills the emotional and intellectual bonds between film and audience. In the hands of a more capable director we could have embarked on a journey of self-discovery and mischief. But in *The Talented Mr. Ripley* we are constantly standing on the sidelines, not able to cheer for either side.

Oh – and Gwyneth was crap and Philip Seymour Hoffman was brilliant … so no change there then.

The Thomas Crown Affair

A bored rich playboy amuses himself by stealing priceless works of art; but has he met his match with the sexy insurance investigator?

Directed	John McTiernan
Writers	Alan R. Trustman, Leslie Dixon, Kurt Wimmer
Starring	Pierce Brosnan
	Rene Russo
	Dennis Leary
Released	1999
Awards	Pierce Brosnan and Dennis Leary won Blockbuster Entertainment Awards, and Rene Russo was nominated for one. The score got a Satellite award and the Hair Styling got a Hollywood Makeup Artist and Hair Stylist Guild Award.
Box office	$124,304,264 (Worldwide)
Tagline	Crime does pay. Handsomely.

"This *Crown*, a smarter and more exciting film than the original, is essentially a two-hour excuse to get this beautiful couple into one compromising position after another…" James Sanford, *Kalamazoo Gazette*, Rotten Tomatoes

Take a very stylish film, starring two of the sexiest stars living (I could almost fancy Steve McQueen myself), and remake it with a plank of wood and a plain Jane. Great idea.

I have nothing against remakes. But surely the idea is to make them better? The all new, low-fat *The Thomas Crown Affair* is a terrible film if taken on its own merits. Brosnan exudes his usual charisma and acting talents – ie. none. I also do not get Rene Russo. Lots of men find her sexy, but I just can't see it. There's nothing about her screams to me screen goddess; she's more like an extra from *Coronation Street*. Together they have little spark (I found the love scenes to be mechanical and sleep-inducing).

If we do compare it with the original then it's in serious trouble. The McQueen/Dunaway version, made in 1968, had a lot of faults, but it just burnt class and style onto your pupils. The split screen, the chess match, the clothes – this was a movie to enjoy and almost get lost in.

McTiernan on the other hand is much more interested in the big va-boom spectacle. This, remember, is the man who brought you *Die Hard* (1988) and *The Last Action Hero* (1993). He's not subtle, and probably doesn't care that his cast can't act (if, indeed, he noticed that there was a cast present).

But for some unknown reason this dog took wings. The world and his wife announced that it was taut, sexy and much better than the original. Sorry, but they're wrong. This isn't a democracy, it's my book. If the rest of the world wants to write one, fine. But until then the overriding opinion of 100% of the writers here say that *The Thomas Crown Affair* is overrated.

Titanic

A penniless artist and a rich young woman meet and fall in love on the *Titanic*. Many are against their relationship (not least her fiancé), but they're on the unsinkable so know they have their whole lives in front of them.

Director	James Cameron
Writer	James Cameron
Starring	Leonardo DiCaprio
	Kate Winslet
	Billy Zane
	Kathy Bates
Released	1997
Awards	You know it won everything going… including 11 Oscars, four Golden Globes, a Grammy for the song etc. etc. 87 awards in total, technical and artistic prizes, and a further 48 nominations.
Box office	$1,835,300,000
Tagline	Nothing on earth could come between them.

"James Cameron has gone and delivered a spectacular, moving, utterly engrossing three-and-a-bit hour epic." Adam Smith, *Empire Magazine*, Rotten Tomatoes

"If you haven't seen it yet, stop reading this instant and run out to the multiplex." MaryAnn Johanson, Flick Filosopher

"… a truly impressive feat of entertainment achieved by Cameron." Almar Haflidason, BBCi

I blame Princess Diana. *Titanic* was heading for disaster faster than you can say "iceberg", with Kate Winslet rumoured to be criticizing it and complaining about the deprivations she had to suffer at Cameron's hands (awful shame love, maybe you should try a normal job instead?). But then the Diana tour of Paris was cut short, and the world decided that an outpouring of emotion was in order. Very shortly afterwards this expensive disaster lumbered onto our cinemas, and instead of laughing it off the screen the general zeitgeist proclaimed it as just the conduit people needed for their tears.

It really was a tragedy for cinema. The biggest grossing film of all time, long-running careers for DiCaprio and Winslet, that blasted theme tune sticking in our heads. Disaster is a word over-used in the modern age, but *Titanic* was a disaster for all of us.

The story is ludicrous, with prim Winslet taking life lessons from someone who looks like a little girl. The set scenes, especially the poor but happy "Oirish" in the bottom deck having a wee dance, the gratuitous topless shot and the pair of them (Kate and Leo, not her body parts) hanging off the front for no apparent reason, are truly dreadful. For such an expensive undertaking the CGI was awful, with the huge liner looking at times as if it was drawn by crayon.

The time dictated that we were allowed to cry; and I think I cried during this more than most (the cinema manager had locked the door). Over three hours' running time is ridiculous, especially as we know that it went down, and the film ends with some selfish old monster throwing the inheritance in the sea (so much for the poor girl looking after her).

To Die For

Suzanne will do anything to be famous, and is happy to eradicate anyone who gets in her way.

Director	Gus Van Sant
Writer	Buck Henry (from Joyce Maynard's book)
Starring	Nicole Kidman
	Matt Dillon
	Joaquin Phoenix
	Casey Affleck
Released	1995
Awards	Nicole Kidman won a Golden Globe, an Empire Award, a Golden Space Needle Award from the Seattle International Film Festival, and four awards from Film Critics Circles. Nominated for a BAFTA amongst others.
Box office	$30,900,000 (Worldwide)
Tagline	She'll do anything to get what she wants … ANYTHING.

"The heroine of Gus Van Sant's deadly funny media satire … isn't just evil with a human face, she's evil with a stunning face and body … Brilliantly written by Buck Henry, *To Die For* works on several levels." Hal Hinson, *Washington Post*

Lots of people love this movie. They call it nice adjectives like clever, smart and funny. But then again lots of people voted for George Bush. There's no accounting for taste. But take my word for it, *To Die For* is not half as smart or sassy as it thinks it is.

The film is obtuse and awkward. Van Sant is desperately floundering around trying to find a tone (it veers from satire to broad comedy and slapstick). Nicole Kidman's performance is easy. Any first year drama student could have come up with the same. The trick would have been to create some ambivalence in the role, make your audience work out who you are, and how far you'll go. In *To Die For*, Kidman is an open book. How the other characters don't realize what she is up to is beyond me.

The storyline is just a little too implausible and contrived to go with. The comedy should have come from recognizing this world, and then realizing in shock that Suzanne will stop at nothing. That doesn't happen here. There is no build up in intensity so we fail to notice the core narrative becoming unlikely. The overblown plot is thrown straight in your face.

To Die For is a terrible movie. It's easy to satirize the media (and you've got the added confidence that the narcissistic press will then love the results). But there is no real intelligence behind the film, nor the controlling hand that makes the difference in good comedy.

Trainspotting

A Scottish heroin addict tries to kick the habit, but what else is there for him and his merry band of friends to do?

Director	Danny Boyle
Writer	John Hodge (from Irvine Welsh's book)
Starring	Ewan McGregor
	Ewen Bremner
	Jonny Lee Miller
	Kevin McKidd
	Robert Carlyle
Released	1996
Awards	The screenplay won a BAFTA, and the film won Best Film and Best Actor at the BAFTAs, Scotland. The score won a Brit. Won four Empire Awards, and two awards at the Seattle International Film Festival. The screenplay was nominated for an Oscar, amongst other nominations.
Box office	$72,001,785 (Worldwide)
Tagline	Choose life. Choose a job. Choose a starter home. Choose dental insurance, leisure wear and matching luggage. Choose your future. But why would anyone want to do a thing like that?

"*Trainspotting* is a singular sensation, a visionary knockout spiked with insight, wild invention and outrageous wit." (uncredited) *Rolling Stone*

Mass hysteria is a terrible thing. A three-year campaign (starting with the book, and then the stage-play, before the film came out) told us basically that we were nobody unless we liked *Trainspotting*. You'd have no street cred, no understanding of "what's really happening out there" (always a phrase that makes me laugh), no feel for modern culture or finger on the pulse. Possibly the biggest brainwashing campaign ever convinced everyone over the age of 14 that this movie was the coolest, most clever and realistic film Britain had ever made.

And it worked – to a certain extent. But, dear reader, I withstood the pressure. With my detached and untrendy eye (not literally – my eye is attached to my body, and eyes have always been more necessary than trendy) I saw through the hype. And what I saw was a pretty average film.

The toilet scene was memorable, the sex montage kinda worked and Robert Carlyle was a revelation as Begbie. But because he was so good it allowed us to see just how ordinary the rest of the cast were. In the lead role Ewan McGregor was lost. For a protagonist Renton had no real character to talk of. Johnny Lee Miller and Kevin McKidd were positively bad.

The big argument at the time was that *Trainspotting* refused to condemn drug taking. This was missing the point. Like the trendy art teacher at school the film was just being disingenuous. It pretended not to take a stand while it was actually really old-fashioned and sanctimonious about the whole thing (look at the film: people crack up, mess up and die because of drugs).

Trainspotting didn't really tell me anything I didn't know. Nor did it show anything I hadn't seen before. It just told Johnny Public that it did, and they naïvely believed the blurb.

Choose life? I'd certainly choose not to have to watch this again.

Training Day

A trainee narcotics detective spends a day with a veteran officer whose methods, not to mention his morality, are corrupt.

Director	Antoine Fuqua
Writer	David Ayer
Starring	Denzel Washington
	Ethan Hawke
Released	2001
Awards	Denzel Washington won an Oscar, and Ethan Hawke was nominated for one. Denzel Washington also won an AFI award for Actor of the Year. Both were nominated for a Screen Actors Guild award, and Denzel Washington for a Golden Globe. It won three Black Reel awards, and was nominated for a number of Film Critic Circle awards.
Box office	Worldwide US$ figure unavailable.
Tagline	In the next 24 hours, you will learn about the streets.

"Good to see Denzel Washington get the meaty villainous role he deserves, and here he luxuriates in the part of Detective Sergeant Alonzo Harris…" Peter Bradshaw, *Guardian*

A terribly bad movie that gets more convoluted and just plain stupid as it goes on. The original premise of the hardened veteran and the wet behind the ears rookie is derivative and unoriginal, but can sometimes be interesting. The film then delves deeper into the old hand's motives and methods, which again could work. But then the whole story goes tits up in an avalanche of "is he or isn't he" nonsense.

Through it all we have to endure Denzel Washington trying to do his best *Hill St. Blues* impression and overacting like hell. How he got an Academy Award for this is a mystery only known to a handful of men. Washington isn't a great actor at the best of times; but here he obviously understands the story as little as we do (and he got to read the script beforehand) and ends up with no idea who his character is or what is really going on. As a two-hander this is not helped by pretty-boy Ethan Hawke obviously settling to just pick up his wage packet with as little fuss as possible. Hawke always gives the bare minimum, but you can see that he's trying to hide behind Washington as much as he can here.

The whole film is pointless and without impact because it tries one twist too many and never really has the confidence of its intentions. The finale really does test incredulity and has to be seen to be believed (actually, no … I've seen it and I still don't believe it).

Les Vacances de Monsieur Hulot

Lovable clown Hulot goes on holidays ... with hilarious consequences.

Director	Jacques Tati
Writer	Jacques Tati
Starring	Jacques Tati
	Nathalie Pascaud
	Michèle Rolla
Released	1953
Awards	It won the Prix Louis Delluc, and was nominated for the Grand Prize of the Festival at Cannes, and for a Best Writing Oscar.
Box office	Worldwide US$ figure unavailable
Tagline	It's laugh-vacation time as Jacques Tati romps through the most gloriously mad lark ever to tickle the ribs of young and old alike!

"There are some real laughs in it, but *Mr. Hulot's Holiday* gives us something rarer, an amused affection for human nature – so odd, so valuable, so particular." Roger Ebert, *Chicago Sun-Times*

Everybody loves Jacques Tati. You're not allowed to call yourself a film fan without swearing allegiance to the French comedian. "This is cinema at its best," they will drone to you, "he was a genius." But the truth is that most "movie buffs" have never actually bothered sitting through this most basic of slapstick. And when they do they are too ashamed to tell their knowledgeable friends that they didn't laugh once for fear of being thrown out of Pretentious Prats Anonymous.

So let's set the record straight, there's nothing funny or inspired about Tati's work (*Les Vacances de Monsieur Hulot* is widely acclaimed as his best – that is if anyone has actually seen any of the others). It is very simplistic and unoriginal clowning, and everyone's now agreed that clowns just aren't funny. Worse, French clowns are particularly not funny. Their attempts at fighting wars are fairly amusing, and their boasts about their food (a good vet could get most meals up and running) and wine (if I wanted to stick my tongue to my mouth I'd use superglue – it tastes better) are hilarious. But French comedians? Come on, we've all endured *Les Visiteurs* (1993), we know that Gallic and humour do not belong in the same sentence.

Tati's work is just lazy, vulgar farce. Genuine genius like Chaplin, Keaton and Arbuckle would have killed to be able to use sound, yet in the 1950s Tati decided to make silent films. Why? Probably because he had nothing funny to say.

I reserve such vitriol for Jacques Tati because without him we would never have had to sit through the unpleasant tedium that was *Sir Henry at Rawlinson End* (1980), Eric Sykes's totally unfunny *The Plank* (1967), and worst of all … *Mr. Bean* (1990).

Vera Drake

A well-meaning amateur abortionist in 1950s London is arrested.

Director	Mike Leigh
Writer	Mike Leigh
Starring	Imelda Staunton
	Richard Graham
	Eddie Marsan
Released	2004
Awards	Won three BAFTAs, six British Independent Film awards, two Evening Standard awards, an Empire Award, a European Film Award and five London Critics Circle Awards, among others. Nominated for three Oscars (Best Achievement in Directing, Best Writing, Best Actress) and a Golden Globe (Best Actress)
Box office	Worldwide US$ figure unavailable
Tagline	Wife. Mother. Criminal.

"It's clear why actors clamour to work with Leigh – this wrenchingly powerful picture has as its lifeblood the kind of performances that don't just happen, they have to be lovingly, patiently nurtured." Wendy Ide, *The Times*

It's hard to think of another post-war film that is more insulting and patronizing to the working classes. For a supposed socialist Mike Leigh should hold his head in shame.

Chirping along like a little cockney sparrow, good old Vera makes sure all her luverley neighbours are OK, and any problems can always be sorted out with a nice cup of tea. She almost offered the audience a cup of tea at one stage. The only thing missing from the clichés was a pearly king and queen, and a good old rendition of "Roll Out the Barrel". Vera Drake? She was more like Charlie Drake.

Vera Drake is a film with little genuine compassion or intelligence. The movie gives no room for discussion or intellectual surmising. Vera was morally right to administer abortions, even though she had no training and little idea who these poor unfortunate girls were. Anyone who has the nerve to disagree with this is just wrong, and a bad person to boot. Leigh's views are rammed in no uncertain terms down the audience's throats with all the subtlety of Leni Riefenstahl.

The film itself has no real purpose except to prove what Leigh knew all the time: that he was right. It is a fairly uneventful if rather infuriating affair. Artistically the piece fails once our lovable Mrs. Mop, played with annoying gusto by over-the-top thespian Imelda Staunton, starts to cry. This occurs only halfway into the picture; and once our love-a-duck, stroll-on, corblimey Vera starts to cry she just doesn't stop (it must have taken her ages to drink her tea).

There's no real suspense as to whether Vera is guilty, or even whether she will be found guilty. Thus the story dies completely, with only an even more patronizing subplot of two stupid poor Londoners falling in love to divert us at all.

The only thing forgotten by Leigh was to cast Dick Van Dyke – but then he would have been too believable.

The Village

A small rural community have an uneasy peace with the creatures that inhabit the surrounding forest, but the fragile truce looks to be coming to an end and everyone will have to face up to their worst fears.

Director	M. Knight Shyamalan
Writer	M. Knight Shyamalan
Starring	Bryce Dallas Howard
	Joaquin Phoenix
	Adrien Brody
	William Hurt
	Sigourney Weaver
Released	2004
Awards	Won an Evening Standard Technical/Artistic Achievement award, and an ASCAP award for Top Box Office Films. Nominated for an Oscar for Best Achievement in Music Written for Motion Pictures, among other assorted nominations.
Box office	$255,395,633 (Worldwide)
Tagline I	Let the bad color be not seen. It attracts them.
Tagline II	Never enter the woods. This is where they wait.
Tagline III	Heed the warning bell, for they are coming.

"In crafting a film about the ways fear can manipulate – are there really creatures of mass destruction in the woods? – Shyamalan gives the film a metaphorical weight that goes deeper than goosebumps. He may find himself linked with Michael Moore as a political provocateur." Peter Travers, *Rolling Stone*

It's OK, I'm not going to tell you the twist. Because you all know there's bound to be a twist. It's an M. Knight Shyamalan picture so there's going to be a twist. He's now more famous for his twists than Chubby Checker, but on the evidence of this spurious twaddle he's unlikely to have the longevity.

I don't need to tell you the twist in *The Village* because it is so obvious that Vera Drake could have spotted it while making the tea. This is a film in which the young director decided to throw as much against the canvas as possible and see what sticks. From *Little Red Riding Hood* imagery to 1984-type discussions on who controls the truth, *The Village* is a convoluted and pointless film.

You've got to feel sorry for Shyamalan. His breakthrough in *The Sixth Sense* (1999) was quite masterful. But now, a little like Slade with the Christmas song, everybody just wants to see him do his little trick again and again.

And so he gets so hung up on an ingenious "ta da!" at the end of the film that he loses all discipline over his narrative and themes. *The Village* isn't ultimately about anything, other than displaying another cinematic sleight of hand. But now everyone is expecting it, and his armoury is not as strong. Critically and commercially he did manage to get away with *The Village* (mostly because everyone was fawning over Ron Howard's daughter for no apparent reason), which is why it merits a listing here, but then came completely unstuck with *Lady in the Water* (2006) (tagline should have been "I can see wet people").

Just goes to show you M., you can fool some of the people some of the time … but eventually they'll get bored (unless you can sing like Slade).

War of the Worlds

As aliens invade earth one regular guy tries to keep his family together.

Director	Steven Spielberg
Writers	Josh Friedman, David Koepp (from H. G. Wells's book)
Starring	Tom Cruise
	Dakota Fanning
	Miranda Otto
	Justin Chatwin
	Tim Robbins
Released	2005
Awards	Dakota Fanning won a Saturn Award from the Academy of Science Fiction, Fantasy and Horror Films, USA, as well as two Critics Circle awards, while Tom Cruise was nominated for a Razzie. The Sound Editing and mixing picked up a couple of awards, and the Sound, Sound Editing and Visual Effects were all nominated for Oscars.
Box office	$591,377,056 (Worldwide)
Tagline	They're already here.

"[Spielberg] returns to his popcorn roots, serving up a voracious big-budget action-spectacular with a pleasingly ravenous bite."
Mark Kermode, *Observer*

Ah, little Tom with his winning smile and subtle head shake. He conquered the world more effectively than any alien could. But this, sadly, was the start of the end. And I mean sadly. Despite his long and (to me) insincere walkabout at premieres (mostly signing autographs that go straight onto ebay) and his annoying dalliances with Katie Holmes (mostly annoying because it's not me snuggling up with her), I do have a lot of time for tiny Tommy. He was possibly the last star that could guarantee to "open" a movie (ie, his name alone would attract an audience), and he also gave us some fine moments among the dross. *Jerry Maguire* (1996), *The Last Samurai* (2003), *Collateral* (2004), *Rain Man* (1988) and, of course, sliding around in his underpants in *Risky Business* (1983) as all teenage boys do the minute their parents leave the house.

But the studios decided they didn't like his religion (would they have been able to do this if he was a Muslim?) and the audiences grew bored with him jumping up and down on Oprah's settee (watch the closing moments of *Scary Movie 4* (2006) to see a great pastiche of this). It's no coincidence that *War of the Worlds* was the meteor that killed his star power. The bigger surprise is that the media had not caught the zeitgeist; strangely many still gave this mess raves.

Were they blinded by Tom's dazzling pearlies? Or perhaps they just presumed that a Spielberg movie couldn't be bad. Whatever it was, the critics saw an entirely different movie from the public (or, at least, the dwindling amount of public who could be bothered).

But there's no mistake about it. *War of the Worlds* is a bad film. The monsters are ridiculous. For some unknown reason Spielberg decides to copy the original's monsters, but then goes his own way with the narrative. Steve, think about it – it was 1957. If the makers of the original could have changed anything it would have been the robots. Tom as a normal blue-collar guy was more alien than the big oil platforms chasing him. There was no real reason for him to go to Boston – the monsters are invading the whole world, so why would they decide to give Boston a break (maybe they're big fans of *Cheers?*).

West Side Story

A modern musical interpretation of *Romeo and Juliet*, with two New York teens from rival gangs falling in love.

Directors	Jerome Roberts, Robert Wise
Writer	Ernest Lehman (from Arthur Laurents's play)
Starring	Natalie Wood
	Richard Beymer
	Russ Tamblyn
	Rita Moreno
Released	1961
Awards	Won 10 Oscars, including Best Picture and Director, three Golden Globes including Best Motion Picture – Musical, and a Grammy for the soundtrack, among others. Ernest Lehman won an award from the Writers Guild of America.
Box office	Worldwide US$ figure unavailable
Tagline	The screen achieves one of the great entertainments in the history of motion pictures.

"The Full Meal Deal – a movie so strong in so many different areas that it's impossible to argue with the 'all-time classic' label that it's been given." Brian Webster, *Apollo Guide*

It may not be pretty or witty, but it's certainly gay. *West Side Story* is the lamest attempt to do anything with Shakespeare ever to hit celluloid. *Romeo and Juliet* is steeped in violence, bitterness, passion and teenage love. Baz Luhrmann showed how to update the piece, and make it relevant to young people around the world, without even changing the lines.

In *West Side Story* all we get are two of the lamest gangs ever seen (even at the age of five, when I first had to suffer this rubbish, I could see that neither the Jets nor the Sharks could fight their way out of a paper bag). The dance numbers go on interminably, without ever realizing that they've outstayed their welcome, and the songs are not as good as everyone seems to think ("America" especially is simplistic, repetitive and irritating – much more like a radio jingle than a classic musical number).

All that money and effort, yet *West Side Story* was never properly transferred from the stage. This is not really a movie, it is a film of the theatrical show, where some of it happened to be shot outside. The makers seemed to have forgotten that they were working within a different medium here. *On the Town* is a film musical, *South Pacific* is a film musical, *West Side Story* is a musical that was filmed.

Withnail & I

Two out of work actors try to escape the city and go for a holiday in the country, to find that things there are much worse and that they are not equipped for rural living.

Director	Bruce Robinson
Writer	Bruce Robinson
Starring	Richard E. Grant
	Paul McGann
	Richard Griffiths
	Ralph Brown
Released	1987
Awards	The screenplay won an Evening Standard Award.
Box office	Worldwide US$ figure unavailable
Tagline	You are invited to spend an hilarious weekend in the English countryside.

"Amongst a slew of cult films which have become the standard fare of the British student, *Withnail & I* towers over all of them, laughing and pointing until it falls over dead drunk." Rich, Mutant Reviewers from Hell

You forget just what a critical smash this was at the time. Everyone loved *Withnail & I*, even if many had real trouble remembering the deliberately difficult title. But, a little like my good self, it has not aged well. And suddenly the vacuous storyline and artistic pretensions are all too obvious.

A second look clearly shows how average the film really is. Writer/director Bruce Robinson was soon caught out: his truly dreadful next picture (*How to Get Ahead in Advertising* (1989)) was completely trashed and he's hardly made a movie since.

Withnail & I survives by the skin of its teeth through spirited performances from Richard E. Grant, Paul McGann, Richard Griffiths, and Michael Elphick, who try their level best with terrible material.

The characterization is poor and stereotyped, the storyline is drab and empty and there's simply no laughs in the whole movie (go on, name one now). The film was taken to the bosoms of students who think they're more intelligent than they actually are. Some even tried to make *Withnail & I* cultish, but it never succeeded on the same level as, say, the Python films.

My overwhelming feeling on second viewing was that of disappointment. Disappointed that I could have been duped so easily and disappointed that I wasn't actually entertained. This film is one of the greatest con acts cinema has ever seen.

X-Men

A team of superhero mutants fight renegade mutants who do not want to live in harmony with humans.

Director	Bryan Singer
Writers	Bryan Singer, Tom DeSanto, David Hayter
Starring	Hugh Jackman
	Patrick Stewart
	Ian McKellen
	Famke Janssen
Released	2000
Awards	Six awards from the Academy of Science Fiction, Fantasy and Horror Films, USA, and four nominations. Two Blockbuster Entertainment Awards for James Marsden and Rebecca Romijn, an Empire Award for Best Director, and several nominations including one for a Hugo for Best Dramatic Presentation.
Box office	$294,100,000 (Worldwide)
Tagline	Join the evolution.

"It's snappy, snazzy, witty, non-exclusive and there are some great performances, with newcomer Jackman – an Aussie stage performer – the standout." Ben Falk, BBCi

Oh good, another comic book adaptation. And this time there's lots of superheroes, all with different powers, and most of them are young and attractive. Talk about covering all bases. *X-Men* is little more than a cynical exercise in selling merchandise, brought to you by the "genius" who made us sit through the horrendous *Apt Pupil* (1998).

I hate to break the spell, but *X-Men* really isn't any good. There are too many characters, with too many attributes, to really concentrate. The special effects are second rate, and after three of the movies I still can't quite work out what they're fighting for and the others are fighting against.

The whole exercise turns into little more than a game of paper, rock, scissors; with the makers just constantly making up another superhero power that can nullify the last one. Thus the film goes round and round in circles not realizing that when everything is possible nothing is special.

And certainly not special is Hugh Jackman who plays Wolverine. *X-Men* really launched Jackman, and for that they should feel very guilty. Not the liveliest of performers at the best of times (watch him snooze his way through *Swordfish* (2001) to see what I mean) he really looks as if he just couldn't be bothered here. The others, including Ian McKellen (who might be gay, but doesn't like to talk about it) and Patrick Stewart play along gamely, although you get the feeling that they don't know what's going on either.

Young Adam

A young drifter gets a job on a barge, but his links to a recently discovered dead body and a dalliance with the captain's wife cause tensions on board.

Director	David Mackenzie
Writer	David Mackenzie (from Alexander Trocchi's book)
Starring	Ewan McGregor
	Tilda Swinton
	Peter Mullan
	Emily Mortimer
Released	2003
Awards	Four BAFTAs – Best Film, Director, Actor, and Actress. Best New British Feature at the Edinburgh International Film Festival, and a London Critics Circle prize for David Mackenzie as British Newcomer of the Year. Various nominations also.
Box office	Worldwide US$ figure unavailable

"It's a dreamy, disquieting study of sexual tension and guilty secrets ... impressive, accomplished work from Mackenzie, who is showing himself to be a natural film-maker." Peter Bradshaw, *Guardian*.

It's hard to imagine a more pretentious pile of arthouse bilge than *Young Adam*. David Mackenzie has been tipped as a rising star for years upon years for no apparent reason (have a look at *The Last Great Wilderness* (2002) if you don't believe me), and *Young Adam* proved beyond a doubt that there's no beginning to his talents.

The film is small in scope and ambition. But when answers are needed to questions about plot or character the director merely throws in more complications to put the audience off the scent. This is a story about nothing, with little to watch (and please fast forward through the horrible custard scene – that's a bird's eye view that no one wants).

The director seems to believe that lots of silences (perhaps he would describe them as moments of dark intensity) makes the film interesting and intelligent. To me it just emphasizes the shallow and pointless nature of the whole exercise. The performances are all fairly lazy except for Peter Mullan, who understands the difference between subtle screen acting and simply standing there doing nothing.

Ewan McGregor has never been the greatest of actors, but at least he can hide behind bravado in the Hollywood blockbusters. Here he looks distinctly uncomfortable, trying desperately to convey information without speaking (a bit like Lassie when someone ends up down the well, but Lassie is better at it).

The visuals are depressing, the sex scenes will put you off your dinner (and definitely your dessert) and the story goes slower than the barge (and never gets to its destination). All in all, a work of genius!

The Oscars

The annual American Academy Awards are generally seen as a definitive list of the best movies of the year. Don't be fooled – this is where films become totally overrated for no apparent reason (the old buffers voting are rarely open to new ideas, and will usually go for the safe option).

The big surprise in the 2006 awards was when *Crash*, quite rightly in my opinion, walked off with the most prestigious award, Best Picture. So maybe they are getting better, but their sins are there for all to see.

Top 5 Movies that Received Seven or More Nominations and Didn't Win One
1 *The Shawshank Redemption*
2 *Double Indemnity*
3 *Broadcast News*
4 *Ragtime*
5 *The Insider*

Top 5 Movies that Didn't Win Best Picture Oscar (that year's winner in brackets)
1 *Citizen Kane* (*How Green Was My Valley*)
2 *The Wizard of Oz* (*Gone With the Wind*)
3 *Singing in the Rain* (*The Greatest Show on Earth*)
4 *Sunset Boulevard* (*All About Eve*)
5 *It's a Wonderful Life* (*Best Years of our Lives*)

Overrated Movies by Number of Awards
1 *Titanic* (11)
2 *The English Patient* (9)
3 *Gone With the Wind* (8)
4 *Mary Poppins* (5)
5 *The Aviator* (5)

Top Ten Underrated Movies

Just to put the list into context, here's my list of the most underrated films of recent times – movies that perhaps just weren't pretentious enough to grab the attention.

The Castle
1997, Directed by Rob Sitch

A small Melbourne community fight the decision to knock down their ramshackle houses to extend the airport runway. I challenge anyone to nominate a funnier film. Shot on a shoestring, this film was chosen to play at the open-air cinema by Sydney Opera House on the night Australia celebrated 100 years of Federation. The comedy is hilarious, and comes from dialogue, action and situation. The characters are warm and lovable, and the catchphrases will stick in your mind for ever.

Curious George
2006, Directed by Matthew O'Callaghan

An explorer comes back from Africa with a disappointing artefact, not the expected centrepiece that would save the museum. He is also followed back by an impish young monkey who he can't get rid of. There are few family movies that can hold a candle to *Curious George*. It plays to all ages without ever appearing boring or immature. Will Ferrell and Drew Barrymore really convince and amuse (George never speaks, but still steals your heart), and there's a great Jack Johnson soundtrack.

Elling
2001, Directed by Peter Næss

Two completely different mental patients are released into the community together, and they must rely on each other to cope with life. This is *The Odd Couple* taken to the nth degree. A Norwegian comedy (sounds like an oxymoron) *Elling* pulls no punches with either character's mental illness or the consequences of their peculiar idiosyncrasies. But the film drags you into their world and suddenly you are lost in the unlikely charm and fun of the situation.

Footloose
1984, Directed by Herbert Ross

A city boy moves to a small town where rock music and dancing have been banned by the local preacher (who is also the father of the girl he adores). *Footloose* is the film that reminds you what it was like to be 18. Every boy gets a girl, the sun always shines, and grown-ups throw out objections to your every (reasoned) point. A great soundtrack (Kevin Bacon actually plays the theme tune when his band play live) and some fantastic set piece dance scenes all add to the best teen movie of all time.

George of the Jungle
1997, Directed by Sam Weisman

After a plane crash George is brought up in the jungle by a wise, and very sarcastic, ape. One day he saves a beautiful young woman from a lion and suddenly he is in love. For comic timing and running gags there are few movies to beat *George of the Jungle*. The film has ten times the sophistication and intelligence of some of the adult "classics" listed in the main section. Its genius is to make a well structured, warm and charming (and hilarious) movie seem apparently simple.

Kiss Kiss, Bang Bang
2005, Directed by Shane Black

A thief gets a movie role, but his reunion with an old girlfriend leads him into a tangled web of intrigue and murder (and incompetence). There are varying degrees of being underrated. You might have heard of this, but perhaps have not seen it. Run to the DVD store now, your life will be much the better for it. Not an Oscar nomination in sight despite having one of the smartest scripts ever written. Val Kilmer deserves an award just for revealing such hidden talents (especially his comic timing).

Local Hero
1983, Directed by Bill Forsyth

An American oil executive is sent to a small cove in Scotland to buy up the land for a refinery, but is charmed, seduced and fooled by the locals and the magic of the area. Loved on its release, *Local Hero* has sadly been forgotten about now. The film deserves another viewing. It has not dated one bit (in fact it is more topical than ever with the ecological debate still raging). This is a film that can make you laugh, cry, and just feel warm about the world – exactly what a good movie is supposed to do.

Manhunter
1986, Directed by Michael Mann

A serial killer is on the loose and an FBI agent, whose mind-blowing speciality is to get inside the brains of killers, is dragged back onto the job. It's not that *Manhunter* did not receive its plaudits, but the fact that it was swept away by *Silence of the Lambs*. Don't be put off with Hammy Hopkins; this was the original and the best Hannibal Lecter movie. Possibly the scariest movie ever made (I literally did search behind the curtains). Brian Cox will blow you away as the killer.

Sahara
2005, Directed by Breck Eisner

An explorer goes to Africa in search of a lost Civil War battleship, and encounters a beautiful UN doctor who is being hounded by the country's dictator. It is unbelievable how this classic was cruelly overlooked by critics and public alike. The film has wit, sex appeal and a knowing wink to the audience that never becomes tiresome or smug. Matthew McConaughey is a fantastic actor, and with *Sahara* he found the perfect vehicle for his charm and wit. Go see it, you won't be disappointed.

Saved!
2004, Directed by Brian Dannelly

In a fundamentalist Christian community a young girl becomes pregnant and learns the truth about who's essentially good in her High School. This is one of the cleverest teen comedies to come out of the States for years. Produced by REM frontman Michael Stipe, the genius of *Saved* is that it never actually takes the mickey out of Christianity, just out of fundamentalism. Adhering to high school comedy strictures it almost reinvents the genre. Worth seeing just for Macaulay Culkin in a wheelchair.

Sources

Apollo Guide
http://www.apolloguide.com

Austin Chronicle
http://www.austinchronicle.com

BBCi
http://www.bbc.co.uk/films

Boston Globe
http://www.boston.com/movies

Britmovie
http://www.britmovie.co.uk

Campus Nut
http://www.campusnut.com

Chicago Sun-Times
http://rogerebert.suntimes.com

Christian Science Monitor
http://www.csmonitor.com

Christian Spotlight on the movies
http://www.christiananswers.net/
spotlight/movies

Culture Vulture
http://www.culturevulture.net

Dallas Morning News
http://www.dallasnews.com

Decent Films Guide
http://decentfilms.com

Detroit News
http://www.detnews.com

EFilmCritic.com
http://www.efilmcritic.com

Empire Movies
http://www.empiremovies.com

Entertainment Weekly
http://www.ew.com

FilmCritic.com
http://filmcritic.com

Flick Filosopher
http://www.flickfilosopher.com/
blog

The Guardian/Observer
http://film.guardian.co.uk

Groucho Reviews
http://www.grouchoreviews.com

Imdb Newsgroup Reviews
http://reviews.imdb.com/Reviews

Imdb Pro
https://secure.imdb.com

Los Angeles Times
http://www.calendarlive.com/
movies

Manly Men's Movie Reviews
http://morpo.com/movies

MetaCritic
http://www.metacritic.com

Metro Times Detroit
http://www.metrotimes.com

Movie Habit
http://www.moviehabit.com

Movie Reviews UK
http://www.film.u-net.com

Mutant Reviewers From Hell
http://www.mutantreviewers.com

Newsday
http://www.newsday.com/
entertainment/movies

The New York Times
http://www.nytimes.com

Not Coming to a Theater Near You
http://www.notcoming.com

The Onion A.V. Club
http://www.avclub.com

Ozus' World Movie Reviews
http://www.sover.net/~ozus

Plume Noire
http://www.plume-noire.com/
cinema

Premiere Magazine
http://www.premiere.com

Reel.com
http://www.reel.com

Rochester Democrat and Chronicle
http://www.democratandchronicle.
com

Rolling Stone
http://www.rollingstone.com/
reviews

Rotten Tomatoes
http://uk.rottentomatoes.com

San Francisco Chronicle/Examiner
http://www.sfgate.com

SciFi Watch
http://www.scifiwatch.com

Seattle Post-Intelligencer
http://seattlepi.nwsource.com/
movies

Slant Magazine
http://www.slantmagazine.com

Spirituality & Practice
http://www.spiritualityandpractice.
com/films

The Times
http://www.timesonline.co.uk

Urban Cinefile (Australia)
http://www.urbancinefile.com.au

Variety
http://www.variety.com

Village Voice
http://www.villagevoice.com/film

Washington Post
http://www.washingtonpost.com

Window to the Movies
http://www.windowtothemovies.
com